The John Ford Movie Mystery

Andrew Sarris

London

Secker & Warburg in association with the
British Film Institute

The Cinema One Series is published by
Secker & Warburg Limited
14 Carlisle Street, Soho Square, London W1V 6NN
in association with the
British Film Institute, 81 Dean Street, London W1V 6AA

General Editors
Penelope Houston and David Wilson

The John Ford Movie Mystery by Andrew Sarris
first published by Secker & Warburg 1976
Copyright © Andrew Sarris

SBN 436 09940 3 (hardcover)
SBN 436 09941 1 (paperback)

Designed by Michael Farrell

Filmset in Photon Times 11 pt by
Richard Clay (The Chaucer Press), Ltd, Bungay, Suffolk
and printed in Great Britain by
Fletcher & Son Ltd, Norwich

Contents

Cover: *Young Mr Lincoln*

Introduction

John Ford was suspected of being an artist long before movie directors became fashionable deities and obsessive objects of *la recherche des films perdus*. My earliest encounter with any kind of directorial dissertation occurred with a pamphlet on Ford in the very early Forties. It was a flimsy pulp by the standards of today's sturdy gloss in the field; nothing much more, I recall, than a collection of reviews gathered from hither and yon with bristling superlatives for *The Informer* and *The Grapes of Wrath*, and sour blasts at *Mary of Scotland* and *Submarine Patrol*. But the overall tone was approval tinged with awe for the bargain Ford had struck with the philistines in the front offices. For every *Informer* he was allowed to initiate, the Mephistophelean mathematics of Hollywood supposedly decreed, Ford was obliged to deliver three *Wee Willie Winkies* to propitiate the gods of the box office.

At the time I had not seen either *The Informer* or *Wee Willie Winkie*, and thus the fable of Ford's forced bargain with Hollywood seemed eminently reasonable and even heroic to my impressionable mind. Years later I was disappointed to discover that *The Informer* was more turgid and more sentimental than its exalted reputation had led me to imagine. A cornerstone of Ford's reputation with the critical establishment had been chipped away in my mind, and the entire edifice of his career tottered precariously from that day forward. I finally caught up with *Stagecoach* and *The Grapes of Wrath* only after I had become enthralled by the wit and verve of Preston Sturges, the Marlovian megalomania of Orson Welles, the sour-sweet-sly romanticism of Billy Wilder, and, above all, the showy

7

technical expertise of Carol Reed. In this context, the foghorn heroics of *The Long Voyage Home* and the barefooted theatrics of *Tobacco Road* struck me as both mannered and manipulative.

In the brave new world of the Forties and Fifties, Ford struck me as a Model-T movie-maker who had run out of emotional and intellectual gas. My late brother once alerted me to an urban cult that celebrated the rustic glories of *My Darling Clementine*, but I never joined that cult, and indeed I was one of the few people in the world who ever really understood why the late Robert Warshow preferred the unheralded *Powder River* to *My Darling Clementine* as a genre treatment of the Wyatt Earp–Doc Holliday legend. And then many, many years after I had first heard of *Wee Willie Winkie* as the price Ford had had to pay for making *The Informer*, I finally caught it on a Shirley Temple series on television.

The joke, then as now, was on the Faustian critics. Despite the monstrous mythology of Miss Temple, *Wee Willie Winkie* contains extraordinary camera prose passages from the wide-eyed point of view of a child. Ford's intuitive framing for maximum expressiveness marked him here, as at the beginning of his career, as a director who could draw pictures on the screen without clogging up the continuity with mere pictorialism. But by the time I saw *Wee Willie Winkie*, I was so committed to John Ford's career that I could only meditate on its remaining mysteries, and they are still many and varied and perhaps even insoluble.

1: Early Days

Very little has been written about John Ford apart from his career, and not very much more about the career itself. From this meagre Ford literature, three works are especially noteworthy, both for their tenacity in treating the director as a serious artist, and for their unconscious reflection in tandem of Ford's shifting reputation through the years. Curiously, all three works are entitled simply *John Ford*, as if the subject were so elemental that no conceivable titular modification could be appropriate. In chronological order, they are by Jean Mitry (1954, revised 1964), Lindsay Anderson (written in 1955 and finally published in the magazine *Cinema* in 1971) and Peter Bogdanovich (1968).

It is now generally agreed that the director was born Sean Aloysius O'Feeney (the anglicized spelling of O'Fearna) on 1 February, 1895 in Cape Elizabeth, Maine. But for many years even the bare facts of his birth and early years were shrouded in the mists of Celtic fancies. Lindsay Anderson addressed himself to this problem in very speculative terms:

The family background is of more than ordinary importance. John Ford's – Sean Feeney's – parents were immigrants; his father was born in Galway, in the West of Ireland, and his mother came from the island of Arran. Sean was the youngest in a family of eleven. Beyond this, we can be sure of very little. For among the Irish traits that have remained influential in his character, Ford has delighted to indulge that fondness for mystification, that evasiveness, half mischievous, half poetic, which seems profoundly a part of the national temperament. And like many Celtic emigrants, and their descendants, he seems to have cherished the traditional habits of his forbears, sometimes to the point of exaggeration. But it is worth remembering that 'Irish' qualities are only an extension of Irish qualities. If they make reliance on Ford's own statement and anecdote somewhat risky, they are also the key to much that is fundamental in him as a man, and as an artist.

Disregarding, then, some latter-day suggestion that Ford was himself born among the green fields of Western Ireland, it seems safest to accept the facts as they have many times been stated in Hollywood press releases: that Sean Feeney arrived on this earth in Maine, in the United States of America. When he was still young, his family moved down the coast to Portland, and there he was able to indulge his boyhood passion for sailing. Other facts are scanty. Whether Sean had any idea of becoming an artist seems doubtful. He wanted to be a sailor. But in spite of his enthusiasm, he failed on graduating from High School to win his appointment to the Naval College at Annapolis. Instead, at the age of nineteen, he went up to the University of Maine. His experience of higher education was, however, brief. Three weeks after his enrolment, he cut loose and made for Hollywood.

Jean Mitry's thumbnail biography includes the information that Ford worked briefly and unhappily in a shoe factory before joining his brother in Hollywood. Ford himself told Peter Bogdanovich that he was the youngest of thirteen children, and not eleven, as Anderson has reported. For his part, Anderson takes playful cognizance of Mitry's account of how Patrick, and later Sean, changed from Feeney to Ford 'in homage, M. Jean Mitry pleasantly suggests, to the English Elizabethan dramatist'. Again Ford himself may have set the record straight once and for all in a Bogdanovich interview on the subject:

Bogdanovich: Why did you and your brother Francis take the name Ford?

Ford: After having worked around in stock companies, my brother went to New York and became stage manager for some company that was going to do a Broadway show; having a very retentive memory, he also understudied four or five parts. The night of the opening, a fellow who was playing one of the important roles – a comedy part – got drunk or broke his leg or something – I think the former. So my brother Frank stepped into the part and made a hit of it. But the name on the bill was 'Ford' – so from then on that was his name – he

Ford directing *The Long Gray Line*

could never get rid of it; neither could I – I was always called Ford. A few years later, a fellow came up to me and said, 'I'd like to have a job – I'm a pretty good actor.' I said, 'You're a good type – what's your name?' He said, 'Frank Feeney.' I said, 'That's very funny – that's my brother's real name.' He said, 'I know – I'm the original Francis Ford – the one that got dru – I mean, broke his leg the night your brother took the part!' I thought it was such a funny gag, I gave him a good part. He changed his name to something else and worked for years. I think he's passed away now.

Ford's garrulous explanation is so much less satisfying culturally than Mitry's that one can understand a film historian invoking the bitter admonition in *The Man Who Shot Liberty Valance*: 'When the legend becomes fact, print the legend.' In a sense, John Ford is himself a legend, and the discrepancies that keep popping up in his various biographies may never be resolved.

A case in point is the biographical sketch that appears in the Wisconsin-based journal *The Velvet Light Trap* in its August 1971 special John Ford issue:

The son of an Irish saloonkeeper, John Ford (Sean Aloysius O'Feeney) was born on February 1, 1895, in Cape Elizabeth, Maine. After completing high school he applied for the U.S. Naval Academy at Annapolis and barely missed acceptance. Ford then spent six weeks at the University of Maine, dropped out, and worked his way out west as a cowboy. In 1913, broke, he decided to go to

Hollywood where his elder brother Francis was already established as an actor-writer-director. He obtained work with his brother and other directors including Allan Dwan, and gained varied experience as an actor, prop man, stunt man, and assistant director before directing his first film in 1917. Ford is now an Admiral in the U.S. Navy.

Certainly, the first eighteen or nineteen years of his life seem completely beyond our reach. Even Peter Bogdanovich was unable to delve into Ford's deepest feelings about his own past via the direct route of the interview. It is only when his own childhood is displaced artistically by Roddy MacDowall's in *How Green Was My Valley* that Ford can fill the gap in his own existence, but only obliquely:

Bogdanovich: Was the family life in *How Green Was My Valley* personal to you?
Ford: Well, I'm the youngest of thirteen, so I suppose the same things happened to me – I was a fresh young kid at the table.

Ford was a man of images rather than a man of letters, and it was thus unlikely that he would ever explain himself adequately in literary-psychological terms. Perhaps that is just as well. Ford knew as well as we do that the supposedly formative years in his life between 1895 and 1913 would not interest us today if it had not been for all the undeniably fruitful years in his career between 1913 and 1966. We seek out the man only because of his movies, and not, as with Stroheim, Welles and even Renoir, the movies because of the man. Within the past decade Ford interviews of varied size, shape and sobriety have appeared in such specialized periodicals as *Cahiers du Cinéma*, *Positif*, *Présence du Cinéma*, *Focus*, *Action* and *Films in Review*. None the less, Ford was one of the most difficult and discouraging interviewees in the business. Lindsay Anderson suffered through an especially disastrous interview with the director back in the early 1950s, but the exchange (printed in *Sequence*) tends less to invalidate Anderson's critical insights than to demonstrate Ford's instinctive resistance to stylistic psychoanalysis. In any event, Anderson's invincible devotion to Ford's art is beautiful to behold in the final flourish of the failed interview: 'As the foregoing has probably made plain, Ford is pretty well interview-proof ... "I want to be a tugboat captain," he says. But God made him a poet, and he must make the best of that.'

How Green Was My Valley (Sara Allgood, Roddy MacDowall)

Kenneth Tynan has described a critic as one who knows the way but can't drive the car, certainly a more charitable description of the critic's calling than most Hollywood directors would accept. In addition to the normal barriers between artist and critic, there is the traditional hostility between West Coast dream merchants and East Coast word-mongers. A continent has usually separated the dream from its deepest analyses, distance lending both enchantment and distrust. On the most provincial level of transcontinental tantrums we find Hollywood's suntanned heartiness arrayed against New York's sallow sophistication, the doers with their physical vitality against the thinkers with their intellectual authority. The chasm between East and West is even wider and deeper for a director who has worked as often as Ford in a genre as culturally disreputable to bookish cliff dwellers as the Western. Ironically, the Western has always been taken more seriously in London, Paris, Rome, Berlin, Tokyo and the other foreign metropolises of myth-making than in New York. One cannot imagine the members of the Algonquin

Circle ever ruminating about the mystique of Monument Valley. And even the late Robert Warshow could not have had many illusions about the number of subscribers to *Commentary* or *The Partisan Review* who had actually seen *Powder River* or even *My Darling Clementine.*

Except possibly for *The Quiet Man,* no John Ford film had either a critical or popular success in New York for the last twenty-five years of his career. To the taste-makers, even in Hollywood, Ford's late-period epic Westerns – beginning with *Fort Apache,* reaching their apex with *She Wore a Yellow Ribbon, Wagonmaster, The Searchers,* and *The Man Who Shot Liberty Valance,* and ending somewhat anticlimactically with *Cheyenne Autumn* – made their grizzled veteran director seem not so much quintessentially American as quaintly archaic. New York represented to Ford not only all the dude critics with their prissy prose, but also all the studio money men with their insensitivity to his most cherished personal projects. Ford did not survive in a cut-throat industry for close to half a century by embracing the world around him. Instead he built walls round himself to keep out the prying intellectuals, desert moats round his film-making locations to discourage the interfering movie moguls, and blinkers round his eyes to keep him from becoming hypersensitive to the stylistic razzle-dazzle of his colleagues.

But the gruff, surly exterior that betokened independence and integrity in the Thirties and Forties sagged with age in the Sixties and Seventies to convey to the disenchanted observer mere indifference and intransigence. For many young people who have no way of knowing and for many older people who should know better, the name of John Ford has come to mean Old Guard politically and old hat artistically. Hence, Randall Poe's front-page article in the *Village Voice* of 16 March, 1972 ('St Patrick's Day '72: The Irish Misconnection') begins with a dialectical flurry at the expense of Ford: 'In the face of Jewish, black, and Italian consciousness, the turn to John Ford's Ireland rather than Brendan Behan's is puzzling.' Mr Poe is obviously more aware of the Ford who brought the vernal greens of *The Quiet Man* to the screen than of the Ford who filmed the vagrant greys of Liam O'Flaherty (*The Informer*) and Sean O'Casey (*The Plough and the Stars*). However, the Ford even of the Thirties would have identified more closely with today's activist wing of the Irish Republican Army than with its ideological wing. Thus perhaps Poe has recognized his real enemy after all; but the point to be made with Ford is that he is too complex an artist to be treated with the crude tools of political dialectics. Moreover, he has meant too many different things to too many different people at too many different times for him to be fished out from the stream of history and mounted as an unchanging archetype. He must be seen in the process of flowing and often merely floating through time, his, ours, the medium's and the world's.

Much of what happened to Ford happens to all old men and all old artists. Much, but not all. It is only when Ford became old that he became fully liberated from the constrictions of his calling. And it is only when he became completely unfashionable that he became completely himself. These are propositions that remain to be argued. Obviously, this book would never have been undertaken if its only purpose was to support the prevailing notion of Ford's artistic decline in the Fifties and Sixties. Jean Mitry has already added a chapter in his book to downgrade the later Ford films and the critics foolish enough to admire them. Nor is there much point in attempting to match Peter Bogdanovich's feat of making Ford the last and greatest monument of Monument Valley. What is needed more urgently at this moment is a bridge between the small band of surviving Ford enthusiasts on the far side of the river and the vast army of nonbelievers and disbelievers on the near side.

As Lindsay Anderson demonstrated consciously in 1952 and as Peter Bogdanovich demonstrated unconsciously in 1968, the director himself could not or would not provide the ultimate solution to the John Ford Movie Mystery. With all the questions put to Ford on the printed page, tape-recorders, film and television, we have in response a record of resistance and evasion that would do honour to the most obscurantist modern artist. The search for a solution must turn therefore from the direct, though reluctant, testimony of the man to the indirect testimony of his movies.

Until very recently the vast majority of Ford's films had not been available for reappraisal since the date of their release. Excluding war documentaries, television serials, cameo, second-unit, acting and otherwise curtailed assignments, there are some 125 titles in Ford's directorial filmography. Of these, sixty-six were released before 1930, and thirty before 1920. A 1969 press release of the American

Film Institute suggests the dimensions of the research problem. Under an underlined all-caps scare headline reading: 'JOHN FORD'S FIRST FILM RESCUED BY AMERICAN FILM INSTITUTE; SEQUENCE TO BE SHOWN ON NBC,' the release goes on to announce: 'The first feature film ever directed by the man generally considered to be America's foremost motion picture director has been "rescued" by the American Film Institute. John Ford directed *Straight Shooting*, starring Harry Carey with Hoot Gibson, in 1917 to begin a career that has grown in international renown over the last half century. The picture, long supposed lost, was tracked down by the American Film Institute which found the only known print in the Czech Film Archive. (It is ironic that numerous American silent features can be found today only in the archives of Eastern European countries.)'

All this fanfare for just one of the thirty-eight films Ford directed for Universal in the silent era. Where are the other thirty-seven? Not at the Universal Studios in Hollywood, certainly. Peter Bogdanovich went through the place with a fine tooth-comb, and all he could find were some production notebooks that established, among other things, that Francis Ford rather than John had directed *The Trail of Hate* in 1917, thus reducing Ford's directorial output that year from nine movies to eight. In 1918 he is credited with seven, and in 1919 with fifteen! Thirty movies in three years, and only *Straight Shooting* has survived the ravages of archaeological irresponsibility. Consequently, the John Ford Movie Mystery begins with a virtual blank on the screen for the first three years in which the director is practising his craft. Nor is it entirely a matter of the passage of time, since we possess infinitely more filmed evidence of D. W. Griffith's career before 1915 than of Ford's before 1920. What little there was in the way of film scholarship before 1930 could not be blamed for placing a much lower priority on Ford *vis à vis* Griffith. The *New York Times*, for example, reviews no John Ford movies made before 1922, and even after 1922 fails to cover *Face on the Barroom Floor*, *Three Jumps Ahead*, *Cameo Kirby*, *North of Hudson Bay*, *Hoodman Blind*, *Hearts of Oak*, *Kentucky Pride*, *The Fighting Heart*, *Shamrock Handicap*, *Three Bad Men*, *The Blue Eagle* and *Upstream*. (Film historians who still blindly trust the microfilmed reviews of the *Times* as the sole arbiter of film history should be made aware of the vast gaps in coverage, particularly where Westerns are concerned.)

16

Straight Shooting

How important is it that we see all of Ford's pre-1920 movies before rendering a final verdict on his career? It depends on what we are looking for. The thumbnail synopses and even the titles of most of these movies sound unprepossessing to a fault. Even the most dedicated film historians might find it difficult to bestir themselves for a revival series of *The Tornado, The Scrapper, The Soul Herder, Cheyenne's Pal, The Secret Man, A Marked Man, Bucking Broadway, The Phantom Riders, Wild Women, Thieves' Gold, The Scarlet Drop, Hell Bent, A Woman's Fool, Three Mounted Men, Roped, The Fighting Brothers, A Fight for Love, By Indian Post, The Rustlers, Bare Fists, Gun Law, The Gun Packer, Riders of Vengeance, The Last Outlaw, The Outcasts of Poker Flat, The Ace of the Saddle, The Rider of the Law, A Gun Fightin' Gentleman* and *Marked Men.* And even if by some miracle of archival resurrection these missing Fords came chugging along, we would still be faced with the problem of comparing the Fords in question with the films of other directors from 1917 through 1919.

For how else can we isolate the unique factor of directorial style from the products of habit, custom and inertia? Here some straight talk on the painful realities of film scholarship is in order. Until very recently most historians in the field have been either unable or unwilling to see many if not most of the movies on which they presumed to pass judgment. A few faded press clippings could provide the necessary synoptic and syntactic hints for a terse notation on a 'minor' work. The more hurried or more 'comprehensive' film historian could simply mention the titles of unseen movies in passing, and even win points for good taste by citing these unadorned, uninflected, unreflected titles as the mnemonics of mediocrity, i.e. unfamiliarity. Thus was ignorance, willed or inadvertent, transformed into a positive virtue. For the most part, film historians have maintained a conspiracy of silence on the pitiful state of archival facilities. When so few in the book business or in academe or even in films either know or care about the shrivelled state of film archives, the temptation is overwhelming for even the most responsible film historian to bluff his or her way through just one more time from what is inferred only indirectly from microfilm to what is expressed directly on a pulsating screen of light and darkness. If I have chosen on this occasion to be candid about the state of my own scholarship, it is not because I wish to confess my inadequacies to the proud possessors of academic astigmatism, but rather because I wish to admit the possibility that it may take many more years to solve the John Ford Movie Mystery.

Auteurism, as it has evolved from François Truffaut's *La politique des auteurs*, places a premium on having seen every work by a director who is deemed worthy of a study in depth; and by the time all the cross-references have been pursued in every possible direction auteurism seems to insist that every film ever made is relevant to the inquiry. And not merely every film, but everything in the air and in the mind contiguous to every film. Hence, authentic auteurism, far from narrowing the historian's focus on film to the dimensions demanded by the frame-by-frame heretics and the stilted structuralists, must inevitably expand into an encyclopaedic awareness of not only the universe of film itself, but also the exact position of film in the universe. It follows therefore that though John Ford's career has crested on many occasions, it cannot be considered apart from the oceanic cinema in which it has ebbed and risen. It is possible also that the darkness in which much of Ford's career is still shrouded has actually contributed to the romantic mystery of his critical reputation. The Man, as it were, Who Came Out of Nowhere. The Artist Who Beat the System. Or better still, the Poet from Poverty Row. Perhaps it is to Ford's advantage to keep his unseen films permanently suppressed. Perhaps in the very footage of the brothers Sean and Francis squared off for one of their family brawls we might find the plastic and kinetic confirmation of powerful feelings only hinted at in all the Ford interviews. And perhaps not. For the moment we must make do with *Straight Shooting*, courtesy of the Prague Film Archive.

There were very mixed reactions to the rediscovery of a 1917 pulp Western like *Straight Shooting* at the 1967 Montreal Film Festival. Archer Winsten, the wearily sophisticated film reviewer of the New York *Post*, chalked off this otherwise inexplicable (to him) exhumation to the peculiar frenzy of FOOFS (Friends of Old Films). Winsten thus remained loyal to an instinctively urban critical sensibility to which the conventions and even the myths of the Western genre have always seemed falsely stereotyped and unimaginatively vulgar. The French-Canadian cineastes on the scene were even more outraged than Winsten was. What had the Ford of 1917 or of 1967 for that matter to do with the reality probes of John Grierson and Jean Rouch, the revolutionary rhetoric of Jean-Luc Godard and Pier Paolo Pasolini, and the cultural, political and economic traumas of French Canada? Ford himself was in attendance along with Jean Renoir and Fritz Lang, and there was a discernible tendency to treat all three of these giants of the medium as the Dead Hand of the Past. Renoir and Lang, like Ford, were represented by 'lost' films (*La Marseillaise* and *Liliom* respectively) which most observers thought should have remained lost. It might be said that Montreal in 1967 rejected the encyclopaedic embrace of auteurism with a vengeance.

The opposite swing of the pendulum takes us all the way to Peter Bogdanovich's scholarly coup of sorts in *Directed by John Ford*, a piece of filmed Fordolatry sponsored by the American Film Institute. With clips of Harry Carey in *Straight Shooting* and John Wayne in *The Searchers*, Bogdanovich captures two actors nearly forty years apart in an almost identical process of expressing the feeling of loss by rubbing and squeezing an arm as if the arm itself had absorbed the pain of parting. Any Ford scholar should be eternally grateful to

19

Bogdanovich for this insight, and for the eye and memory for detail that made it possible. But what of the relatively disinterested, uninterested or even hostile witnesses to Bogdanovich's contribution to Fordiana? If one may take the role of devil's advocate, the fact that a gesture was repeated forty years later may signify nothing more than the freezing of genre acting into conventional patterns. Also, the artistic autonomy of acting may seem to be jeopardized by imposing a bit of business performed by one player on another. That it was right for Carey does not necessarily make it right for Wayne. 'Did Wayne really *feel* it?' the neo-Stanislavskians and mumbling Methodists might inquire in unison. And even this viewer cannot say for sure whether Ford actually invented the gesture in the first place or merely quoted Carey's stylistic contribution forty years later as a conscious or unconscious homage. Besides, the fact that the gesture has now been identified as a directorial figure of style does not in itself establish its aesthetic credentials. Thus, again from the viewpoint of the devil's advocate, Bogdanovich may be said to have indulged in the besetting vice of too many auteurists (myself often included): elucidation without evaluation. Of the Carey–Wayne visual-echo effect, it may be so, but so what?

As it happens, *Straight Shooting* gives us at most merely a tantalizing glimpse of Ford's artistic beginnings. But already we can sense that the forceful images on the screen tend to transcend the feeble ideas behind them. Ford's framing of horsemen sliding down a sandy hill can be traced from *Straight Shooting* to *The Lost Patrol* in 1934 to *The Searchers* in 1956. Even as the narrative continues to move forward from background to foreground, Ford's imagery clutches at the visual memory of the viewer. Here we are at a time when the Western was still relatively new even though the West was old, and the Old West virtually dead, and yet Ford is already casting a sombre spell on the screen, his *mise en scène* already in mourning, his feelings of loss and displacement already fantasized through the genre. This elegiac element in his style helps explain why Ford was spotted as a stylist surprisingly early in his career. It is more than a matter of beautiful pictures. The silent screen was saturated with them. It is rather a matter of the dynamic counterpoint between the physical and emotional energy of his players and the reflective overview of his extraordinarily quiet camera.

20

The stylistic control inherent in this dynamic counterpoint persisted a full half century from *Straight Shooting* in 1917 to *Seven Women* in 1966, without Ford ever losing the equilibrium of his very delicately balanced expression of the twitches of life on the silhouettes of legend. A remarkable feat of directorial fidelity under any circumstances, but especially so in an industry given over so frequently to the fads of the moment. Ford succumbed neither to the wide-screen longueurs of Henry King, nor to the arrogant critics-be-damned archaisms of Cecil B. DeMille; rather, he demonstrated the viability of his classical style well into an era when truth was considered a function simply of lenses and filters. Therefore, the major (if not sole) interest of *Straight Shooting* is its confirmation of a directorial personality. Otherwise, the movie operates on a level of pulp poetics that would concern only the more specialized Aristotles in the genre; that is to say, someone more like William K. Everson than the late Robert Warshow. Thus whereas Warshow lumped together Tom Mix and William S. Hart into a soupy stereotype of the supposedly naïve Western hero of the silent era, Everson (in *The Western*, written with George N. Fenin) establishes a dichotomy between the rodeo antics of Mix and the romantic agonies of Hart.

If we accept this Eversonian dichotomy, *Straight Shooting* and most of Ford's Westerns fit more closely into the Hart mould than into the Mix mould. Harry Carey, the hero of no fewer than twenty-six of Ford's Westerns, was a relatively ragged saddle-tramp by Mix's rodeo standards, often starting out on the wrong side of the law, then being redeemed by the love of a good woman or the sight of a helpless baby or (as in *Straight Shooting*) the villainies of his confederates. Ford and Carey reportedly used to make up many of their movies as they went along, and it is interesting to note how often family ties are more decisive than abstract notions of honour and justice. Indeed, even before the Ford–Carey collaboration began, there was in *Tornado*, probably the first movie Ford directed and one for which he also wrote the script and played the lead, an ending in which the hero (Ford three times over) uses the reward money to bring his'mother over from Ireland.

A little later, when Carey has taken over the acting chores from Ford, there is a profusion of mothers, sisters, wives and sweethearts in a supposedly rootless genre. The studied stoicism which Warshow so admired in the Westerner has little connection with Ford's Irish

21

The elegiac element: *3 Bad Men*

sentimentality. More than a few spectators in Montreal in 1967 were startled by Harry Carey's tears in *Straight Shooting*. The spectacle of a man's sobbing seemed not only unmanly but mythically inappropriate. This apparent incongruity can be explained to the uninitiated in two ways: first, very few 1967 viewers had any idea of what the Westerns between 1898 and 1930 were really like; and, secondly, Ford was demonstrating as early as 1917 that there was a distinction between what he rendered unto the genre in the currency of conventions and what he rendered unto himself in the coinage of feelings.

It would be a mistake, however, to deduce from *Straight Shooting* that Ford had become a conspicuously creative force in the cinema or even the Western as early as 1917. The notion of creativity in cinema has been linked traditionally to Faustian conflicts between high-minded artists and pot-bellied financiers, to radical innovations in technique, and topical breakthroughs in content, and traumatic exercises in candour. The confirmation of creativity has often been of a negative nature: the industry's neglect of Griffith, its nullification of Stroheim, its neutralization of Eisenstein, its niche-placing of Flaherty, and its nit-picking on Welles. Greatness and integrity are thus measured less in terms of cinema than of metacinema, that is not by the films that were actually made but by those which might have been made if conditions in the industry were more conducive to creativity. Ford cannot possibly be considered a master in these martyred terms. He himself noted his lack of resistance to the studio

22

system with the rueful confession to Peter Bogdanovich: 'I can fight like hell, but I always lost.'

Thus it would seem that Ford functioned more as a drifter than as a driver in the very early part of his career. None the less, he was making choices as he went along, regulating the exact direction of his drift to his own temperament. His casting, for example, goes beyond Eisenstein's *typage* (the plastic resemblance of a passerby to the part) to *archetypage* (an actor's behavioural identification with the part). The apparent disdain of variety necessary to use Harry Carey twenty-six times in roughly the same role places Ford at the opposite end of the spectrum from a fastidious director like Robert Bresson, who unearths non-acting types for his leads and then discards them as if they were his own personal drawings up there on the screen. In this way Bresson creates his own myth by annihilating his actors and thereby reducing their faces to their most literal significations. By contrast, Ford always fostered a feeling of amiable continuity in his cinema. Once a player wanders into Ford's world and settles down in it without undue temperament or histrionics, he (and the operative gender is usually he) may return as often as he wishes.

With very few exceptions, Ford's casting is direct rather than devious, allegorical rather than ironical. Hence, Harry Carey never played the villain for Ford, nor for anyone else. Ford not only dedicated *Three Godfathers* in 1949 to his erstwhile star, who had died a year earlier: 'To the memory of Harry Carey – bright star of the early Western sky.' He also provided frequent employment to Harry Carey, Jr, as well as to the children and grandchildren of other members of his repertory company. A Ford set is thus often a community in itself in the process of representing a larger and more lyrical community on the cosmic screen.

In later years Ford was to become identified with (and frequently stigmatized by) the recurring presences of such favourites as John Wayne, Henry Fonda, Victor McLaglen, Maureen O'Hara and Anna Lee, not to mention vintage gargoyles like Dan Borzage and Francis Ford, the latter a fearsomely fraternal projection of the director's Irish irascibility amid a drunken devotion to the cause of some almost forgotten campaign. Ford's willingness to cast and recast his films with his old friends runs counter to the conventional illusionism of the movie industry. Though players, and especially stars, were often typecast in Hollywood movies, the impression was supposed to persist that each role represented a new challenge in a relatively suspenseful situation.

Alfred Hitchcock has often claimed that star casting reduced uncertainty in the narrative since no one in the audience really believed in the fatal vulnerability of, say, Cary Grant. Interestingly enough, it was Hitchcock himself who once proposed to cast Harry Carey in *Saboteur* (1942) as a Nazi agent, a kind of fanatical outgrowth of the America-First-anti-FDR movements in the grass roots. Mrs Harry Carey reportedly vetoed the idea with the admonition that no American boy would ever believe in anything again if Carey were presented as a traitor to his country. Perhaps that is precisely what the impish Hitch had in mind all along. The point to remember is that no such casting idea would ever have occurred to Ford. He was thus never given to intrigue and deception in the development of his plots, and, as we shall see, this artistic tendency seemed to critics and audiences suitably sincere for a time, then doggedly simplistic, and finally downright naïve.

Ford's feeling for tradition makes him especially vulnerable to the tendency in film criticism of upholding variation at the expense of repetition, a tendency encouraged by the bias towards variation in the written words of which criticism is composed. On the whole, Ford's films appeal less to the writer than to the viewer in the reviewer. And most movie reviewers, particularly in the English-speaking countries, are more comfortable around books than around paintings. Significantly, Lindsay Anderson chose to hail Ford as a poet rather than as a painter, even though it was clearly the director's eye rather than his ear that was the source of his sublimity. But with painting, the critic must come to terms with style as a palpable presence on the canvas above and beyond the apparent subject. I am not arguing that the cinema is necessarily closer to painting than to poetry or narrative or drama or music or anything else. I am merely suggesting that there are in Ford's art certain aspects for which literary analogies are inadequate and inappropriate. And among the most notable of these aspects is his ritualized casting as a visual incantation of the continuity of a community. The fact that Ford seems never to have felt his artistic originality diminished by the presence of a familiar face on the set attests to a feeling for the reunion as the dominant goal of all human endeavour.

What is surprising is that Ford has prospered in a pop art context while withstanding with Homeric calm the journalistic demands for perpetual innovation. Not that he ever entirely escaped the studio Cyclops with their one-eyed tastes in story material and performers. A fair number of Ford movies range from undistinguished to diasastrous with, at best, competently neutral direction to keep them off the shelf. And even his most accomplished films are not without serious flaws. The ultimate argument for Ford rests on the ability of an unexpectedly supple talent to transcend flaws in areas of the cinema which failed to excite and involve him. Among these neglected areas is the narrative for its own sake, the story with a twist, the brand new subject, the chic new attitude. Ford's cinema pays a price for this neglect, and it is good that Hitchcock's too often despised showmanship is around to redress the balance. None the less, one would be ill-advised to speculate about the quality and impact of a Ford film on the screen purely from a printed synopsis or even from a period critique. Something extra-magical seems to happen between the synopsis and the spectacle where Ford is concerned. Thus for all the Ford films up to 1930 only a few marginal notes are in order at this still primitive point in film scholarship.

From Ford's pre-1930 period I have now seen in addition to *Straight Shooting* (1917) the following features: *Just Pals* (1920), *Cameo Kirby* (1923), *The Iron Horse* (1924), *3 Bad Men* (1926), *Four Sons* (1928) and *Hangman's House* (1928). Recent exhumations from the Fox archives have made *Napoleon's Barber* (1928) available for viewing, but so far only on the West Coast. *Cameo Kirby* is interesting if only for the reason of its being the first film credited to John Ford rather than the earlier, pulpier Jack Ford. *Moving Picture World* commented: 'Director John Ford has been especially skilful in framing each scene to artistic advantage.' The plot was based on a Booth Tarkington–Henry Leon Wilson play, which Cecil B. DeMille had made into a film back in 1914. Cameo Kirby is a Mississippi riverboat gambler but a Southern gentleman withal. He enters a crooked card game to help an old man who is being victimized, cleans out the victim along with the card-sharps, fully intending to make restitution; but the old man, unaware of Kirby's honourable intentions, commits suicide, complicating Kirby's courtship of the victim's daughter, but not permanently. Jean Mitry regards *Cameo Kirby* as a turning point in Ford's career:

Early work: *Just Pals* (1920) and (*below*) *Cameo Kirby* (1923)

'Après un série de films dépourvus d'intérêt, il réalisa enfin la première oeuvre dans laquelle ses diverses tendances parvinrent à s'équilibrer harmonieusement. Accordant les structures plastiques d'une image recherchée à l'action directe et violente du Western, *Caméo Kirby* marqua le point où l'artiste se révèle à lui-même, où l'artisan s'affirme en accédant à la maîtrise.'

Three years earlier Ford had directed a movie called *Hitchin' Posts* for Universal with very much the same plot and central character as in *Cameo Kirby*. Indeed, the synopsis of *Hitchin' Posts* reads like a minor-studio rip-off from a major-studio property. What is odd is that Ford, in moving upwards in his own career from Universal to Fox, should mimic his ascent by directing a property he had plagiarized, again more the attitude of a painter with a familiar subject than of a novelist with an original plot. It might be noted that *Cameo Kirby* was remade in 1929 under the direction of Irving Cummings, and that this basic plot was the subject of a spoof by Danny Kaye in the strenuously vulgarized 1947 film version of James Thurber's *The Secret Life of Walter Mitty*. And certainly at least vestiges of the character of Cameo Kirby survived for Ford in John Carradine's courtly Hatfield in *Stagecoach*.

According to Peter Bogdanovich, *Marked Men* was Ford's favourite among his early films. Based on Peter B. Kyne's story, *The Three Godfathers*, a movie of that title had been made in 1916 by a forgotten director named Edward J. LeSaint, and with Harry Carey in the lead. Ford remade it in 1919 with Carey, and in 1948 with John Wayne in the Carey part. In the intervening years William Wyler directed a version entitled *Hell's Heroes* (1929), and Richard Boleslavski a much less memorable version entitled *Three Godfathers* (1936). That Ford was caught up so frequently in the remake merry-go-round of the Hollywood studios does not mean necessarily that his style was considered sufficient to lend novelty to well-worn material, but rather that audiences and reviewers had such short memories that the same plot could be trotted out every three or four years with no one being the wiser.

Only very recently have film historians had the opportunity to compare remakes as the acid tests of directorial differences, but it would be a mistake to make too much of such comparisons. The same plot repeated becomes more self-conscious, the same set more traditional, the same director more experienced, the same players

Marked Men

older and more familiar. Hence, the morphology of time alone is sufficient to reshape the most literal remake. When we begin contemplating variations in the other elements of production, the supposed similarities between 'originals' and 'remakes' become minuscule indeed. In writing of the conventional form of the Western, Robert Warshow articulated the aesthetic paradox of the medium itself: 'The form can keep its freshness through endless repetitions only because of the special character of the film medium, where the physical difference between one object and another – above all, between one actor and another – is of such enormous importance, serving the function that is served by the variety of language in the perpetuation of literary types. In this sense, the "vocabulary" of films is much larger than that of literature and falls more readily into pleasing and significant arrangements.'

Still, the voluminous cross-references in Ford's career to other careers may provide useful clues to the director's artistic personality. Thus Ford's *Lightnin'* (1925), with Jay Hunt and Edythe Chapman in the middle-aged leads, might profitably be checked against Henry King's *Lightnin'* (1930), featuring Will Rogers and Louise Dresser. Boxing historians might note that Ford directed no less a personage than James J. 'Gentleman Jim' Corbett in *The Prince of Avenue A* (1920), technically the director's first non-Western, but very much in the spirit of his brawling Irish Easterns. *Gentleman Jim* (1941) with Errol Flynn in the eponymous role turned out to be one of Raoul

Walsh's most graceful romances. Nor should we forget that Ford standby Victor McLaglen once fought Jack Johnson almost to a standstill.

Ford himself evolved out of a ruggedly physical tradition in film-making, both as a stunt man and as a pioneer in location shooting, and the flourish of fisticuffs was treated as a sign of manhood to the end of his career. In both *The Quiet Man* (1952) and *The Searchers* (1956), the outcome of a fight is explicitly linked to the decision in the marriage bed. But Ford's enactments of hand-to-hand combats were always less painful than percussive, less savage than ceremonial. I doubt whether all Ford's screened fist-fights put together could equal the tissue-tearing brutalities inflicted in the circus combat between Åke Gronberg and Hasse Ekman in Ingmar Bergman's *Sawdust and Tinsel* or in the Mexican tavern tempest pitting Humphrey Bogart and Tim Holt against Barton MacLane in John Huston's *The Treasure of the Sierra Madre*. With Bergman and Huston the inflicting of pain and humiliation takes precedence over the celebration of manhood, and the spectacle of suffering becomes the visual symptom if not indeed the vital centre of the human condition. With Ford pugnacity is all, and punishment nil.

For all the films he made up to 1930, Ford's cast lists fail to cause many mythic reverberations even for the most encyclopaedic movie buff. Hoot Gibson (from *The Soul Herder* in 1917 and many films thereafter), Tom Mix (*Three Jumps Ahead* and *North of Hudson Bay* in 1923) and Tom Santschi (*3 Bad Men* in 1926) are of interest mainly to aficionados of the pulp Western. Ford may have had something to do with the 'inside' Hoot Gibson joke in *Mr Roberts* (1955). J. Farrell McDonald pops up everywhere, but he is one of the most remarkably resilient Irish character actors in the history of the movies, and slightly antedates J. M. Kerrigan in the matter of Celtic omnipresence. Eugene Pallette (*North of Hudson Bay*) makes a rare appearance in a Ford film in the midst of an extraordinarily buoyant career, and Henry Walthall briefly reunites the worlds of D. W. Griffith and John Ford in the reportedly bathetic *The Face on the Barroom Floor* (1923). A viewing of John Gilbert's portrayal of *Cameo Kirby* for Ford does not prepare us for Gilbert's star-rocketing performance for King Vidor in *The Big Parade* two years later. By 1930 John Wayne (*Hangman's House* in 1928), Ward Bond and Stepin' Fetchit (*Salute* in 1929) had already appeared in

Hangman's House: John Wayne in his first Ford film

their first Ford films, but the threat to Ford's ultimate critical reputation from the political backlash they inspired was still a very long
way off.

As might be expected, the actresses are fairly marginal creatures
in Ford's masculine cosmos. Seena Owen in *Riders of Vengeance*
(1919) might be worth a look as a foretaste of her bizarre performance for Stroheim in *Queen Kelly*, Barbara Bedford in *The Big
Punch* (1921) as a reminder of her glowingly perverse anti-Griffith
performance in Maurice Tourneur's *The Last of the Mohicans*, and
Irene Rich in *Desperate Trails* (1921), Bessie Love in *The Village
Blacksmith* (1922), Jean Arthur in *Cameo Kirby* (1923), Janet
Gaynor in *The Shamrock Handicap* and *The Blue Eagle* in
1926, Belle Bennett in *Mother Machree* in 1928, Louise Fazenda in
Riley the Cop in 1928, Myrna Loy in *The Black Watch* in 1929,
and Helen Chandler in *Salute* in 1929, all simply for retroactive
reference to a future fulfilled. And we have barely scratched the
surface.

It is perhaps reflective of the area of greatest continuity in Ford's style that he should settle more steadily on cinematographers than on scenarists. Of the thirty-eight movies he made for Universal, no fewer than twenty-two were photographed by John W. Brown, and another six by Ben Reynolds. Of the twenty-eight Fox films with which he was involved, sixteen were photographed by George Schneiderman, and another five apiece by Charles G. Clarke and the legendary Joseph H. August. On the first-hand evidence available to date, Ford's visual style seems to have become somewhat more Germanic and less Griffithian through the Twenties. (For that matter, Griffith's did too.) But the issue seems somewhat more complicated today than it did just a few years ago, when the total representation of Ford silents in the repertory of the Museum of Modern Art consisted of *The Iron Horse* (1924) and *Four Sons* (1928).

With the former film shot on location in Nevada, and the latter shot on a Fox set, it is not surprising that *The Iron Horse* should evoke Flaherty and *Four Sons* Murnau. After all, it would be as hard to be expressionistic out on the open range as it would be to be naturalistic against painted backdrops. Still, *The Iron Horse* and *Four Sons* do happen to constitute in their obvious oppositions a visual dialectic in Ford's style which was to remain unresolved to the end of his career. None the less, this dialectic of day and night, sun and shadow, Manifest Destiny and Implacable Fate, would not be worth discussing in the context of two films as artistically undeveloped and as psychologically unexplored as *The Iron Horse* and *Four Sons* if Ford's career had not taken the strange turns it did after the coming of sound. One must remember also that film techniques proliferated more rapidly in the Twenties than in any decade before or since. And at the time of *Four Sons* particularly, a misty German night was falling over the sunlit screen of D. W. Griffith. Indeed, Murnau's *Sunrise*, the climactic masterpiece of studio expressionism, had been shot at Fox the year before *Four Sons*, and it would have been unusual for Ford *not* to have been influenced by the German master of camera *mise en scène*. Although, as William Everson has wryly remarked, Fox paid for its losses on *Sunrise* with the profits from its Tom Mix movies, there is no question that Murnau and his colleagues at UFA had profoundly affected Hollywood thinking on what a film should look like.

'A visual dialectic': *Four Sons* and (*below*) *The Iron Horse*

For his part, Ford never became enamoured of Murnau's conspicuously expressive camera movements, which were later to be refined and extended by Max Ophüls and Kenji Mizoguchi. Indeed, Ford's camera remained relatively quiet throughout his career even in as supposedly mobile a genre as the Western. Jean Mitry noted this paradox in Ford's style long before it was critically fashionable to isolate directorial figures of style apart from their appropriateness to story content. And it was therefore Mitry who was able to deduce that even in Ford's supposedly epic Westerns like *The Iron Horse* and *Stagecoach*, the illusion of kinesis was created not through gratuitous camera gyrations, but through functional camera followings of the odysseys of the conveyance (locomotive, stagecoach) in each instance.

This form of functionality has been designated by André Bazin as 'invisible' camera movement, and it is present occasionally even in the work of an artist as radically alien to the mystique of the moving camera as Yasujiro Ozu (*vide* the bus ride of the old couple in *Tokyo Story*, not to mention the – for Ozu – curiously lyrical expression of the void in their lives with a brief track along the river bank). Ultimately, invisible camera movement (masked by the movements of persons and objects) like invisible editing (masked by the dramatic logic of a scene) is the mark of a classical tradition of unobtrusive technique. Unobtrusive but not static. Again, Mitry makes the right stylistic association when he relates Ford's dynamism to Sternberg's in that both directors possessed the flair to fashion compositions that burst with movement and excitement within their frames. And both directors were capable of creating graceful pictures without artificial poses.

It has been the happy faculty of the best French film aestheticians to be able to link the Louvre to the Cinémathèque that has enabled them to abstract visual forms from their narrative contexts, and thus discern stylistic resemblances between directors as disparate as Ford and Sternberg. Of course, this Gallic preoccupation with style can be carried to such extremes that individual films are reduced from aesthetic experiences to mere notations in a dictionary of directorial mannerisms. Ford and Sternberg differ, of course, in the recurring themes of their respective story materials. And movies, as we have mostly come to know them, have been marginally rather than maximally abstract. Hence, it would be a mistake to suggest that Ford's movies before 1930 are in any way equal to Sternberg's or, for that matter, to the best of Ford's own movies after 1930. Why? Simply because Ford, unlike Sternberg, had not yet found narrative structures worthy of his talents.

Again, even the most interesting of Ford's 1920s movies do not compare very favourably with the better films of that decade, even in the more facile areas of romance and sentiment. One may note in conjunction with Ford's *Just Pals* (1921) the more affecting achievement of Frank Borzage's *Lazybones* (1925), with a similar theme (the troubles of the town loafer) and the same actor (Buck Jones). Whereas in Ford's film the hero's troubles are finally solved by a flurry of unconvincing melodramatics in the brashest serial manner, the loafer in the Borzage film becomes the tragic victim of his own lack of emotional nerve. Still, *Just Pals* is lovely round the edges, with its last vestiges of Griffithian-naïve deep focus capturing the incidental backgrounds to the story in all their sculpted sincerity. The deep focus of this vanished era was naïve only in the sense that it was not a calculated Welles–Wyler–Toland reaction against the starry-eyed soft focus which attended the perfection of panchromatic film stock in the late Twenties. Here again, deep focus, naïve or sophisticated, is a more nebulous field of inquiry than even André Bazin ever imagined. One of the most extraordinary examples of sophisticated deep focus photography occurs in an otherwise mediocre 1929 Metro musical entitled *Devil May Care*. None the less, the evolution from *Just Pals* to *Four Sons* seems to correspond to the transition between Griffith and Murnau.

If Ford's career had ended in 1929, he would deserve at most a footnote in film history, and it is doubtful that scholars would even bother excavating too many of his Twenties works from the Fox vaults. However, a few marginal observations are in order even in this primitive period of film research. Ford can be very profitably studied before 1930 purely in terms of studio policy. In his years at Universal (1917–21), only two of Ford's thirty-eight feature films did not qualify as some sort of horse opera: the James J. 'Gentleman Jim' Corbett vehicle, *The Prince of Avenue A* (1920), and a mock melodrama (imitative of the five-times filmed *Seven Keys to Baldpate*) entitled *The Girl in Number 29* (1920). By contrast, Ford's output at the fancier Fox studio between 1920 and 1929 consisted of five Westerns and twenty-three non-Westerns. It might be noted also that in the stylistically formative period between *3 Bad Men* in 1926 and *Stagecoach* in 1939, Ford did not make a single Western.

It is thus at the very beginning and at the very end of his career that Ford can be considered primarily a director of Westerns. In between he worked on a variety of more fashionable genres, though generally in the realm of robust romance. And even Ford's 'Westerns' tended to overlap into incongruous regions, periods and genres. One Harry Carey Western (*The Wallop*, 1921) begins with the hero looking at a movie and noticing that the girl sitting next to him is an old flame. Another (*Cheyenne's Pal*, 1917) begins with the startling premise that a cowboy, down on his luck, would regretfully sell his horse to an English quartermaster for service in the trenches of France, and then, repenting, rescue his 'pal' from almost certain death.

Ford's Westerns were therefore quite often contemporaneous with the world he knew first-hand. Ford himself would ride back and forth between the studio and the outdoor locations, and he knew people with eye-witness knowledge of Wyatt Earp and Wild Bill Hickok. Towards the end of his career Ford's Westerns would therefore refer to the Old West not merely as a segment of social history and legend, but also as a personal memory of early film-making. That Ford's Westerns encroached so effortlessly on the modern world suggests also that there was no barrier of stylization between the characters in a Ford Western and the characters in a Ford non-Western. The same distinctive mixture of realism and romanticism, humour and heroism, which flowed through Ford's Harry Carey and Hoot Gibson Westerns flowed also through the showbiz settings of *Jackie* and *Upstream*, the travails of a Jewish family in New York's Lower East Side (*Little Miss Smiles*), the familiar tensions of the big horse-race (*Kentucky Pride*, *The Shamrock Handicap*), the big fight (*The Fighting Heart*), the Army–Navy game (*Salute*), maternal love (*Mother Machree, Four Sons*), paternal remorse and sacrifice (*Hoodman Blind, Hearts of Oak*), family honour in old Erin (*Hangman's House*), gangland rivalry (*The Blue Eagle*), and prohibition shenanigans (*Riley the Cop*).

For the kind of boisterous action ethos to which he drifted instinctively, Ford collaborated surprisingly often in the Twenties with woman scenarists – Frances Marion, Dorothy Yost, Lillie Hayward, Gertrude Orr and Marion Orth. But this seems strange only if we overlook the too often forgotten tradition of womanly vigour in the movies of the silent era. America was still largely a rural, immigrant, pioneering nation with many sagas of family struggle and fortitude, and the Fox studio, through both its William J. Fox and Darryl F. Zanuck periods, tended to reflect this inspirational attitude towards the American experience. When the Fox output is compared to that of Paramount, Metro and First National, one finds at Fox less evidence of the jazz age, of the successive stages of 'continental' comedy reflected in the works of Cecil B. DeMille, Erich von Stroheim, Ernst Lubitsch, Malcolm St Clair, Harry D'Arrast et al. Both Ford and Fox did not have to discover the underdog in the Depression; they had been looking at the world largely from his point of view all through the roaring Twenties. Not with prophetic class hatred, to be sure, or with any serious doubt about the validity of the American Dream, but simply with an uncondescending concern for little people with remarkably modest objectives.

Of course, it is impossible to tell what would have happened to Ford if he had been compelled to direct Rudolph Valentino or Greta Garbo. Would his cultural sensibility have expanded or would his creative feelings have shrunk? Probably, he would have walked away from these uncongenial encounters without having compromised his basic commitment to the continuing epic of wanderers in long shot. Indeed, Ford complained to Peter Bogdanovich of the studio's insertion of a dozen close-ups of Madge Bellamy into *The Iron Horse* (1924) after the completion of shooting. Ford was to endure the same indignity from the same studio twenty-two years later with Linda Darnell's jarring close-ups in *My Darling Clementine*. The flaws remain in both films to mark the occasional submissiveness of an otherwise proud and resolute product of the studio system. And only the most knowledgeable connoisseur of Ford's directorial personality can detect the cracks in the crystallized camera style.

2: 1930–1939: The Storyteller

It is almost too chronologically appropriate that Ford's first film of the Thirties – *Men Without Women* – marks also his first collaboration with Dudley Nichols, a screenwriter with whom he was to be subsequently associated on *Born Reckless* (1930), *Seas Beneath* (1931), *Pilgrimage* (1933), *The Lost Patrol* (1934), *Judge Priest* (1934), *The Informer* (1935), *Steamboat 'Round the Bend* (1935), *Mary of Scotland* (1936), *The Plough and the Stars* (1936), *The Hurricane* (1937), *Stagecoach* (1939), *The Long Voyage Home* (1940) and *The Fugitive* (1947). The Ford–Nichols relationship, especially in the Thirties, is therefore a crucial aspect of any assessment of Ford's developing reputation. In this respect, *Men Without Women* was more important at the time than it has seemed since. It is interesting to note that neither Jean Mitry nor Lindsay Anderson had seen the film when they wrote their studies of Ford. I have seen only a silent print intended for foreign language markets, and thus I cannot fully evaluate it as a talking movie of its time, but I do sense in it a turning point in Ford's career – not the last or even most decisive turning point, but one that seems to have eluded most film historians.

Even the title of the movie signals the path Ford was to follow to his greater glory. Thus, Men without Women implies Man without frivolous distractions or Hollywood conventions. No Madge Bellamy or Linda Darnell close-ups. No fade-out kisses. No rides to the rescue. No concessions to matinee audiences. Of course, a movie about fourteen men trapped in a submarine with an ever-dwindling supply of oxygen was hardly the stuff of an actress's dream. Yet though Ford himself was no stranger to male-oriented scenarios, never before had a Ford film been endowed so elegantly with life-and-death suspense. The directorial turn of the screw here probably did more to enhance Ford's standing as a serious artist than all the grosses from *The Iron Horse* and *Four Sons*. It wasn't merely that *Men Without Women* made several critics' ten-best lists, and lingered in many moviegoers' memories. The unconventional nature of the achievement gave Ford an aura of individuality at a time when anonymity was the lot of most directors. And it helped smooth over Ford's hitherto bumpy transition to the talkies.

Nichols himself recalled that stormy era in a letter to Lindsay Anderson:

I landed in Hollywood in June, 1929. I had earlier finished ten years journalism in New York (reporting, drama criticism, music criticism, columning, one year on a roving assignment in Europe) and had cut my journalistic ties to go on with fiction and other writing ... Winfield Sheehan, then executive head of Fox films, talked me into coming to Hollywood. Sound had arrived and writers were needed. I knew nothing about film and told him so. I had seen one film I remembered and liked, Ford's *The Iron Horse*. So I arrived rather tentatively and experimentally, intending to leave if I found it dissatisfying. Fortunately, Sheehan assigned me to work with Ford. I liked him. I am part Irish, and we got on. I told him I had not the slightest idea how to write a film script. I had been in the Navy during the war, overseas two years, and we decided on a submarine story. I told him I could write a play, not a script. In his humorous way he asked if I could write a play in fifty or sixty scenes. Sure. So I did. It was never a script. Then I went on the sets and watched him break it down into filmscript as he shot. I went to rushes, cutting rooms, etc., and began to grasp what it was all about. But I must say I was baffled for many months by the way Ford could see everything through a camera – and I could not ... Working with Ford closely I fell in love with the cinema ...

Men Without Women is divided into two very unequal parts, the first – virtually a prologue – consisting of a nocturnal prowl in and out of Shanghai waterfront dives. The point of view tends to be collective rather than individualized, the vaudeville almost forebodingly half-hearted. There is a Man with a Past, and another man inquiring into that past, but the two actors involved (Kenneth

Men Without Women: 'the point of view tends to be collective'

MacKenna, Paul Page) look too much alike to establish much dramatic tension. (A talking print might have established idiosyncratic distinctions in their voices.) As if to counterbalance the impendingly claustrophobic stasis of the *mise en scène* inside the doomed sub, Ford made the Shanghai sequences more mobile than was his custom. As Nichols recalled the episode in question: 'They believed long dolly shots could not be made with the sound camera. He did it – one long shot down a whole street, with men carrying microphones on fishpoles overhead.'

Once aboard the sub, the barely introduced characters plunge to their dire destiny without much ado. The bulk of the film is taken up with the physical details of their ordeal. The beauty of Ford's direction is that he orchestrates a veritable symphony of fearful expressions without resorting to the showy cross-cutting of anguished angles. We see fear interacting from face to face within a fixed, communal frame. Stuart Erwin's luminously oafish radio operator is particularly memorable as a fixed point of tension in the midst of intermittent flurries of movement and feeling. On the surface of the ocean, the rescue ships poke through the expressionistic mist of night and fog to plumb the Orphic depths. It is a mood of romantic despair which was to mark the Ford–Nichols collaboration through the Thirties and into the Forties.

However, their collaboration did not achieve its legendary status until the mid-Thirties. And by then *Men Without Women* had receded into limbo. It has never been revived publicly in all the years since. Fox films were always the hardest to research, as Warners were always the easiest, which is why most standard film histories have more of an emphasis on Warners than on Fox. If *Men Without Women* had been better preserved and remembered, the next Ford film – *Born Reckless* – would have seemed like a disastrous setback for the Ford–Nichols team.

By any standard, *Born Reckless* is one of the worst movies ever to come out of Hollywood. Dudley Nichols' screenplay was adapted from the novel *Louis Beretti* by Donald Henderson Clarke, a writer of mildly racy melting-pot romances in and out of the urban underworld. Ford and Nichols seemed completely baffled by the assignment. The scenario appears to point in a different direction with each scene, at one moment towards gangland retribution, at another towards the regeneration of a rogue, at still another towards the preservation of ethnic family honour on the altar of spaghetti machismo. The movie ends in such confusion and indecision that the audience is never quite sure whether Louis Beretti ultimately dies of his gunshot wounds or is allowed to recover. Indeed, the movie never really ends. It simply stops, as if the last day of shooting had arrived before the plot could be tidied up. Even Ford's instinctively impeccable camera set-ups are plagued by glaring spatial and directional inconsistencies in the erratic sequencing of the scenario. It would seem that the director and the scenarist were simply marking time on a hopeless project.

None the less, Ford's own recollection of *Born Reckless* (to Bogdanovich) provides a significant clue to the ultimate direction of his career: 'It wasn't a good story – something about gangsters – and in the middle of the picture, they go off to war; so we put in a comedy baseball game in France. I was interested in *that*. In those days, when the scripts were dull, the best you could do was to try and get some comedy into it.'

As it happens, the baseball game in *Born Reckless* does not redeem the disorganized narrative around it. But the game does release communal feelings which Ford could not find in the gangster genre. Of course, we have no way of knowing what would have happened if Ford had found himself at Warners instead of Fox, and had been assigned *Little Caesar* with Edward G. Robinson or *The Public Enemy* with James Cagney. Edmund Lowe in *Born Reckless* was hardly the equivalent of a Robinson or a Cagney. He was more the good-looking, tough-talking slicker of *What Price Glory* and its many sequels than an implacable force of merry malignancy. Lowe was coming to the end of his brief vogue as a roguish adventurer. He didn't read lines well enough to compete for long with Cagney and Robinson and the Tracys (Lee and Spencer). Lee Tracy supported Lowe in *Born Reckless*, and Spencer Tracy made his screen debut later that year in *Up the River*, a prison film Ford later claimed to have rewritten extensively with William Collier, Snr., from an allegedly solemn screenplay by Maurine Watkins. *Up the River* also marked the first screen appearance of Humphrey Bogart, and thus in iconographical interest alone it towers over *Born Reckless*.

Again we have the big, comical, communal baseball game as a centrepiece for the scenario, but this time Ford has achieved a more interesting balance between the comedy and the roguery. Indeed, it is the very broadness of the comedy which makes the chivalric sentimentality palatable. *Up the River* thus anticipates *My Darling Clementine* and *Wagonmaster* and *The Man Who Shot Liberty Valance* in the treatment of sacrifice as an act of communal devotion rather than as a manly flourish of life style. Already in 1930, Ford seems closer to Renoir than to Lang in his response to genre conventions. By contrast, Howard Hawks' *Scarface* is much closer to the determinist designs of Lang than to the existential escape hatches of Renoir and Ford.

Even the very debatable 'humour' of Renoir and Ford can best be appreciated as a function of their compassionate humanism in the face of a tragic vision of life. At their worst, Renoir and Ford delay the inevitable and the inexorable with the clumsiest vaudeville routines imaginable, Renoir with roly-poly animal acts out of an Impressionist's zoo, and Ford with an Irish bar as a backdrop for the only stage on which death can be deferred in the wings. To put it another way, if Renoir and Ford often soar beyond genre conventions, they equally often sink beneath them. Hence, *Up the River* can no more be compared with *The Big House* or *The Last Mile* than *French Can Can* can be compared with *The Bandwagon* or *Singin' in the Rain*. The most meaningful link in each instance is not between works in the same genre, but between works by the same *auteur*. But it is possible to argue that transcending a genre is merely a noble way

Up the River (Spencer Tracy)

of betraying it, and that Ford and Renoir pay a high price to the medium for the individuality of their visions.

After *Up the River*, Ford did not work with Spencer Tracy again until *The Last Hurrah* in 1958. Tracy's early Thirties Fox career (before he was lionized at Metro) is relatively unfamiliar even to most film historians. Hence, there is something misleading in the traditionally solemn view of the elder Tracy, in whose reformed features the indomitable granite jaw firmed up the sensual leprechaun lips and steadied the guileful Irish eyes of the rascals he played in such undeservedly neglected early Thirties movies as *Up the River, Quick Millions, 20,000 Years in Sing Sing, The Power and the Glory* and *A Man's Castle*. Tracy, in tandem with Warren Hymer, a goofy gangster type of the period, immediately took hold on the screen as a comic rascal. Humphrey Bogart, by contrast, seems disconcertingly callow in his mama's-boy-victim-of-circumstances characterization. His film career was to stutter until he returned to Hollywood in 1936 from his Broadway hit as Duke Mantee in *The Petrified Forest*. Ford never worked with Bogart again, but as with Tracy more as a matter of different studios and genres than of differences in temperament.

Ford and Nichols were reunited in 1931 on *Seas Beneath*, a curious World War I naval project told from the point of view of both the American Q-boat crew and the German U-boat crew under siege by the American vessel. There are espionage plot elements embodied most conspicuously in a treacherous Latin American temptress named Lolita (Mona Maris). But Ford's main complaint about the project was the studio's imposition of an actress named Marion Lessing, of whom nothing was ever heard again. Despite the salt spray of authenticity from the first-hand immersion of the movie in its maritime setting, *Seas Beneath* lacks the dramatic tension of *Men Without Women*. The intrigues on land take too much time with too little conviction, and the divided point of view, so fashionable in this era of pacifist forgiveness, seemed to conflict with Ford's own emotional commitment to the American naval community. Another oddity of *Seas Beneath* is its relentless bi-linguality, with the German dialogue translated by English intertitles rather than subtitles. One of the German officers is played by John Loder, who was to feature more prominently in such future Ford films as *How Green Was My Valley* and *Gideon of Scotland Yard*. George O'Brien, who had played the romantic lead in Ford's *3 Bad Men* and in Murnau's *Sunrise*, played the American Commander in *Seas Beneath*, and, according to Ford, performed his own stunts on a sea too turbulent for professional stuntmen. *Seas Beneath* was remade in 1959 by Dick Powell with Robert Mitchum in the O'Brien role and Curd Jürgens as his German counterpart. The action was updated to World War II, and despite some Good-German–Anti-Nazi contortions, the remake was more effectively entertaining than the original.

Of *The Brat* Ford himself would say nothing except that two of the actresses so loathed each other that they prolonged a squabble in the script beyond the running time of the camera. The screenplay credits tell the whole story – Sonya Levien, S. N. Behrman, Maude Fulton from a play by Maude Fulton, credits appropriate for a Lubitsch or a Cukor, perhaps, but not for a Ford. Consequently, the film has virtually disappeared from film history. The inter-class Pygmalion antics of the plot revolve round the premise that a writer of the *haut-monde* (Alan Dinehart's MacMillan Forester) would reach down into the gutter of night court to appropriate a street urchin (Sally O'Neil's The Brat) for purposes of research for a novel of the lower depths. The Family, attired in all its upper-class regalia, objects to the experiment at first, but love and scruffy virtue prevail in the end.

This 'Peg o' My Heart' material is expertly directed by Ford, even though its talky elegance is not exactly his cup of tea. The cast is only

Seas Beneath, and (*below*) *The Brat*

moderately interesting even for trivia fanciers. Sally O'Neil is another of the forgotten faces of the period; Virginia Cherrill, eternalized if not immortalized as Chaplin's flower girl in *City Lights*, did not linger long in the limelight. Frank Albertson (The Brat's juvenile love interest in the Forester family) was a memorably callow male ingénu with a high-pitched wail for all occasions. Still, the most intriguing of all the players is Alan Dinehart, a mature, slightly corpulent, glib, parasitic confidence man type, a kind of cross between Jack Buchanan and Edward Arnold. He generally posed as a man of the world, but his place in it was always less secure than that of an Adolphe Menjou or a Herbert Marshall. He remained a minor figure in the iconography of the Thirties, but even so he was completely extraneous to the vision of John Ford.

After a decade at Fox, Ford was borrowed by Samuel Goldwyn to direct *Arrowsmith*, with a prestigious cast headed by Ronald Colman, Helen Hayes, Richard Bennett and Myrna Loy, an even more prestigious script by Sidney Howard from the novel by Sinclair Lewis, and a score by Alfred Newman as an added guarantee of success. Ford made the most of his opportunity by demonstrating the ability to tell a wordy story in a sequence of crisp, forceful images. *Arrowsmith* was the kind of socially oriented property in which the players could be kept at a reasonable focal distance. Colman and Hayes did not engulf the screen with high-powered close-ups. The film was not really about their subjective insights so much as about their objective idealism. The ill-fated Leora of Helen Hayes is an especially poignant character because we see her so often in modest long shots as if she could never be more than a small part of her husband's obsessive concerns. Her compulsive smoking as a symptom of her pent-up passion seems to survive in such later Ford neurotic heroines as Maureen O'Hara's tormented wife in *Wings of Eagles* and Anne Bancroft's mannish doctor in *Seven Women*. It is to Ford's credit that he understood intuitively the frustrations of his female characters, even if he lacked the imagination to remedy them.

None the less, *Arrowsmith* remains basically a scriptwriter's movie with a theatrical climax in Ronald Colman's stirring integrity speech before the final fade-out. There were many such speeches in the idealistic Thirties, notably Edward G. Robinson's in *Five Star Final*, John Barrymore's in *Topaze*, Walter Huston's in *Law and Order*, Paul Muni's in *The Life of Emile Zola*, Robert Donat's in *The Citadel*, and of course, to round out the moral aspirations of the decade, James Stewart's veritable flood of rhetoric in *Mr Smith Goes to Washington*. Ford did not entirely escape wordy scripts during the decade, but for the most part his style came to be defined by the implications of images rather than words. Hence, it was not the speech itself, however eloquently written or delivered, which revealed Ford's attitude, but the visual spin-off from the speech. In *Arrowsmith*, it is Colman turning forcefully to the audience as if to ask challengingly: Where do we all go from here? It is at this precise moment that Ford's instinctive preference for lucidity over

Arrowsmith

ambiguity becomes apparent. This was later to become a stylistic issue
between Ford and Wyler, especially for such French aestheticians of
the Fifties as André Bazin and Roger Leenhardt. But 1931 is too
early for such speculations; John Ford has not yet become John
Ford in the eyes of the fashionable critics of that period. One might
note in this respect that neither John Grierson nor Dwight
Macdonald bothered to mention Ford in their erudite directorial
round-ups of the early Thirties.

Nor did Ford's subsequent films in 1932 and 1933 enhance his
reputation to any appreciable extent with the taste-makers of the
period. *Air Mail* (1932) marked Ford's return to his first studio,
Universal, with a moody, foggy saga of the early days of air mail
flying. It is the kind of good movie which, in its time, was dismissed
because of genre prejudice. Unfortunately, *Air Mail* does not seem to
have been available when the New Critics of *Cahiers du Cinéma* and
Movie were resurrecting Hollywood's action ethos of the Thirties for

Air Mail

highbrow auteur and genre revaluations in the Fifties and Sixties. Consequently, the misty aircraft movie genre tends to be identified almost exclusively with Howard Hawks because of *Dawn Patrol* (1930), *Ceiling Zero* (1936) and *Only Angels Have Wings* (1939), and deservedly so. *Air Mail* is not as fully or as finely articulated as Hawks' treatment of this romantic material. Curiously, *Air Mail* and *Ceiling Zero* share the same scenarist (Frank W. Wead) and virtually the same plot, and yet the two movies diverge decisively mainly because of two contrasting directorial visions. Again, Ford's is the view from long shot, submerging the squabbling egos of the pilots in cameraman Karl Freund's luminous contemplation of the plane itself as the communal vehicle of all the hopes and fears of the characters. By contrast, Hawks' celebrated eye-level viewpoint concentrates on the aerial/Ariel aspirations of the fliers themselves, and reduces the planes to bird-like appendages of the presumptuous groundlings.

Frank W. ('Spig') Wead worked with Ford thirteen years later on

They Were Expendable, and then became the heroic subject of Ford's *The Wings of Eagles* some twenty-five years after *Air Mail*. Still, the script of *Air Mail* comes over today as little more than a first draft for *Ceiling Zero*, which was a hit on Broadway before Hawks transferred it to the screen. Interestingly, Pat O'Brien, who played the roistering daredevil to Ralph Bellamy's benignly restraining influence in *Air Mail*, became, in turn, the benignly restraining influence to James Cagney's roistering daredevil in *Ceiling Zero*. As much as anything, O'Brien's transition from the romantic role to the responsible one marks also his evolution from a rebellious lead of the second magnitude to a respectable support of the first magnitude. *Air Mail* is notable also for the debut of legendary stunt flier Paul Mantz, who later lost his life in an air accident during the production of Robert Aldrich's *The Flight of the Phoenix* (1966).

Why Ford chose to move on to Metro-Goldwyn-Mayer to do a sordid Wallace Beery vehicle entitled *Flesh* (1932) must remain one of the unsolved mysteries of his career. The crowded writing credits – scenario by Leonard Praskins and Edgar Allen Woolf from a story by Edmund Goulding (director that year of the Oscar-winning *Grand Hotel*) with dialogue by Moss Hart – suggest frantic conferences to whip up a feasible concoction for the fans of Beery's very beery earthiness. Here the burly character lead plays a German wrestler who journeys to America where he is victimized by a gangster (Ricardo Cortez) and his eventually repentant moll (Karen Morley). Beery's is the kind of role Jannings might have played if he had remained in Hollywood after the coming of sound. Cortez, one of Garbo's most memorable leading men (in *The Torrent* of 1926) and the screen's first Sam Spade, was reunited with Ford twenty-six years later as the Jewish district leader in *The Last Hurrah*. Karen Morley was very much the Vera Miles of the Thirties in that her manic wistfulness in morbid rôles (*Scarface, Dinner at Eight, Our Daily Bread*) made her a memorable presence of the period without ever making her a star. (The comparable roles for Vera Miles were in *The Wrong Man, The Searchers, Psycho* and *The Man Who Shot Liberty Valance*.)

Ford returned to Fox in 1933 after a three-picture absence to make *Pilgrimage*, one of his biggest commercial successes up to that time. Again, as with *Four Sons*, Ford capitalizes on the inherent sentimentality in the loss suffered by a war mother, and again it is

I. A. R. Wylie who provides the original story material (in this instance a story entitled *Gold Star Mother*). Philip Klein and Barry Connors were credited with the scenario, with dialogue attributed to Dudley Nichols. By any standard, *Pilgrimage* is a disconcerting project to associate with the Ford–Nichols integrity legend. First, the studio is all wrong. Ford and Nichols were later to make their reputations at RKO, whereas Fox always represented for Ford's critics the siren call of convention and compromise. Also, *Pilgrimage* looks back not merely to the maternal sentimentality of *Four Sons*, but to some of the worst excesses of the windswept melodramas of the silent era. The opening sequences are particularly egregious as Henrietta Crosman's jealous mother turns her son (a callow, wild-eyed Norman Foster, brother of Preston, and later nominal director of that Wellesian whirlwind *Journey Into Fear*) in to the draft board to save him from the clutches of an especially angelic Heather Angel. The son is killed in the War to end All Wars, and his sweetheart bears his child, and cares for it in proud poverty, but the mother remains unforgiving and unrepentant as the wind howls through the trees on Fox's back-lot of rural America.

How will Henrietta Crosman's Hannah Jessop see the error of her ways? Simply by making a pilgrimage along with other Gold Star Mothers to her son's final resting place in France. There she will fortuitously encounter another young man with another monstrous mother in exactly the same situation with which *Pilgrimage* began. From this mirror re-enactment, Hannah Jessop finds the wisdom to avert a second tragedy, and to reconcile herself to her responsibility for the first by acknowledging at long last her daughter-in-love and grandchild as her very own flesh and blood.

So much for the scenario and its ridiculous contrivances. The bulk of the film is another matter. Ford and Nichols do not merely transcend their material, but skilfully subvert it by shifting the emphasis from the mechanics of the plot to the mood of an epic voyage of stoically Trojan mothers to the graves of their slain warrior sons. This shipload of maternal pride and sorrow is thus analogous as a communal conveyance with mythic overtones to *The Iron Horse* and the submarine in *Men Without Women* and the plane in *Air Mail*, which preceded it, and to the *Steamboat 'Round the Bend* and the *Stagecoach* and the overloaded Okie truck in *The Grapes of Wrath*, the fog-shrouded freighter in *The Long Voyage Home*, the

Pilgrimage: 'stoically Trojan mothers' (Lucille Laverne, Henrietta Crosman)

doomed PT-boats in *They Were Expendable* and the exultantly congregational covered wagons in *Wagonmaster*, which followed. And, again, Ford's discreet camera distance, and his behavioural doodling on the margins of the scenario, create epic feelings without bombast or pretension. Especially memorable is Mrs Hatfield (Lucille Laverne) with her corn-cob pipe, hillbilly high spirits and womanly stoicism. But she too finally submerges herself in the ranks of one of John Ford's many unconventional armies.

Although *Pilgrimage* was a great box-office success, especially at New York City's Radio City Music Hall, John Ford's name had still not quite penetrated the critical consciousness, and it was not uncommon for Ford's films to be reviewed without even a mention of their director. This pattern of directorial anonymity became even more pronounced when Ford ventured into *Doctor Bull*, the first of three projects he shared with Will Rogers, then the reigning star of the Fox studio and an authentic American legend in his own right. Born William Penn Adair Rogers on 4 November, 1879, in the Indian Territory that was later to become Oklahoma, he died on 15 August, 1935 in a plane crash which also took the life of the celebrated flier Wiley Post. Rogers, part Indian, had been a cowboy, a soldier in the Boer War and a Wild West show performer before hitting Broadway with a lasso-slinging act interspersed with *ad lib* comments on the state of the world. His talent as a roper has been preserved on the screen in three of his films – *The Ropin' Fool* (1922), *Ambassador Bill* and *The Connecticut Yankee* (both 1931). Although he was appearing in movies from 1919 on, his greatest success came in the talking era. He was the middle-aged twangy star of twenty-one movies in little more than half a decade, and he helped keep Fox afloat until Shirley Temple could toddle to the rescue. In addition to his movies, the cracker-barrel persona of this quintessential American was purveyed in newspapers, lectures and radio broadcasts.

Here then was a screen presence with an iconographical identity established long before Ford had made his mark, and yet his three films with Ford – *Doctor Bull* (1933), *Judge Priest* (1934), *Steamboat 'Round the Bend* (1935) – are strikingly different from his work with other directors. Ford, more than any of the others, surrounds the star with a social context in which he fits very snugly despite his shot-prolonging off-beat improvisation. Indeed, Ford often sacrifices the personality of this adventurously *ad lib* performer to the balanced framing of evocative images of an old order dying slowly with its ageing protagonist. By contrast, Frank Borzage's *They Had to See Paris* (1929) and *Young As You Feel* (1931) elicit the richest feelings from Rogers as a creature of the here and now. The Borzage films are especially interesting today because we are in the midst of rediscovering the behavioural beauties of the Thirties, beauties that were too long obscured by a pedantic concern with abstract forms and social themes. Whereas Borzage brings out the pleasure-seeking side of the Rogers persona, Ford illuminates a devotion to duty. With Borzage, it is a matter of Rogers having a last fling. With Ford, it is a matter of Rogers making a last stand.

Not that Will Rogers wasn't in a decisive sense the major auteur of all his movies. The same man left the same tracks in film after film, but the better directors kept him from wandering off to the land of nodding self-indulgence, the ultimate task, after all, of any director. Still, it is interesting that Ford never tapped some of the more topical aspects of the Rogers persona to be found in such overtly political movies as *Ambassador Bill* and *County Chairman*. Nor was the Ford–Rogers collaboration as deviously anti-city-slickerish as the James Cruze–Rogers collaboration on *Mr Skitch* and *David Harum*, nor as leisurely with its spinning of homespun wisdom as the Henry King–Rogers collaboration on *Lightnin'* (a Ford project in the silent era) and *State Fair*.

51

Rogers was not quite the biting satirist subsequent legends have made him out to be. His Middle American populism was relatively mild even for its time. In Rogers, iconoclasm wrestles an often losing battle with philistinism, and, not infrequently, populism is smothered in the pieties of the plutocrat. The good-natured gibes at Jewish accents (though not in any of Ford's films) may seem more sinister after Hitler than they were meant to be before. Still, there is something undeniably refreshing about Rogers today. For one thing, he always acted his age. A man in his fifties, he never pretended to more potency than he felt, and yet he never hesitated to be generous with his dwindling assets. He was less a lampooner than a lamplighter of the virtues and vices of a kind of archetypal American. He was remarkably open to the world, open to learning and to travel. (His death in flight was perhaps not as accidental as it seemed.) It would never have occurred to him to apologize for being an American, but he was too much the fractious Democrat ever to wave the flag in a dully Republican manner. It was part of his shrewdness to allow himself to be deceived to his own advantage in the personal power game, but then neither Camus nor Sartre ever confronted the dialectical dilemma of being a rich movie star in a starving world. The collected cinema of Will Rogers is therefore more interesting as history than as allegory or even as nostalgia. More than most movie stars, Rogers tended to record the times in which he lived, and most of his films were conceived and executed in the present tense. This makes it all the more remarkable that Ford was able to project Rogers so hauntingly into the past tense.

Of the three Ford–Rogers projects, *Doctor Bull* was the first in time and the least in impact. Adapted by Paul Green from an early novel (*The Last Adam*) by James Gould Cozzens, and with additional dialogue by Janet Storm, the script lacks the rich thematic texture of the Dudley Nichols–Lamar Trotti scripts for *Judge Priest* and *Steamboat 'Round the Bend.* As a cranky Connecticut country doctor, Will Rogers spends most of the time outraging the community with the somewhat aimless antics of an ageing rebel without a cause. There is a relaxed romance with a friendly widow (Vera Allen) and a dramatically redemptive epidemic and the familiar generational crisis of sweet young things stifled in their innocent love by stuffy old fools. Doctor Bull is afflicted also by the unfriendly competition of Ralph Morgan's mod Doctor Varney, a PR physician of test tubes and testimonials in the spirit of Jules Romains' *Doctor Knock*. But the movie is little more than the sum of its digressions, and the leisurely pacing seems more appropriate for turn-of-the-century Kentucky than for turn-off-the-turnpike Connecticut.

And yet Ford successfully imposes a distinctive sensibility on his meandering material by establishing the social co-ordinates of his milieu with an expressive panning shot which, in effect, circles the town square from sidewalk to steeple, and thereafter serves as the communal context for all the characters. To translate into spatial terms Doctor Bull's commitment in time to his merry widow, it is sufficient for Ford to show in very distant long shot the doctor's old roadster parked outside the widow's home on an autumnal carpet of fallen leaves. None the less, it seldom if ever occurs to anyone that Ford was a New Englander by birth, a Down-Easter to be more precise. Ford's Odyssey, both physical and spiritual, took him West and South, and, most often, backwards in time. And yet East or West, Ford focused on what is most enduring rather than what is most ephemeral; he never left the small neighbourly town lodged in his mind.

Between *Doctor Bull* and *Judge Priest*, Ford made *The Lost Patrol* and *The World Moves On*, and between *Judge Priest* and *Steamboat 'Round the Bend*, he made *The Whole Town's Talking* and *The Informer*. Hence, there has been a tendency for Ford's Will Rogers movies to get lost in the shuffle. *The Informer*, especially, so completely outshone every other Ford achievement in the critical consensus of its time that there has been a tendency ever since to downgrade the supposedly solitary pre-eminence of this instant classic. Unfortunately, Ford's other films of the period were never particularly accessible either for revival or for television. Hence, as we look at Ford's Thirties' movies with the benefit of hindsight, we recognize a much more diversified aesthetic than was commonly acknowledged at the time.

Judge Priest is especially interesting in this regard because of its unresolved conflict between what Ford had been and what he was to become. (Also, *Judge Priest* was less remade than reshaped some twenty years later into *The Sun Shines Bright*, an expanded and deepened version of Ford's 1934 meditation on life and politics in a small Kentucky town still divided in 1890 by memories of the Civil War.) Will Rogers does not so much play Judge Priest as loosely

Will Rogers as *Doctor Bull* and (*below*) *Judge Priest* (with Stepin' Fetchit)

inhabit him through a series of leisurely Irving S. Cobb stories adding up ultimately to a form of anecdotage on the front porch of My Old Kentucky Home. The days bask in the lazy conviviality of small town life a while or so back, but the nights are full of fear and foreboding and death as the yelping of bloodhounds is heard across the land. It is mostly mood, of course. The plot is too confused and congested to follow a clean line in any direction, and the slapdash melodramatics of the courtroom trial (complete with vindicating flashback memories of cavalry charges in the Civil War) go back beyond *Birth of a Nation* to the contrived theatrics of plays like *The Copperhead*. As if to evoke the lingering influence of D. W. Griffith on Ford, it is the Little Colonel himself, Henry B. Walthall, who plays the key role of remembrance in the courtroom drama of *Judge Priest*.

But what is most memorable in *Judge Priest* is the scene in which the eponymous protagonist visits his wife's grave and talks to it as if he were making a regular report on the life lingering just slightly beyond her ken. Ford endows this one-way conversation between the living and the dead with more emotional resonance in such later Orphic enterprises as *Young Mr Lincoln* and *She Wore a Yellow Ribbon*. Here in 1934 Will Rogers tosses off the scene with a reading that seems, for once, too loosely improvised and too prosaic for the metaphysical rigour of the poetic conceit. And Ford's camera treatment and cutting seem unduly tentative, if not actually embarrassed. Possibly, Ford was too aware of the widespread critical distaste for funeral parlour cinema through the Thirties. It was a decade in which people talked to pictures, statues, headstones and other mementoes from the Great Beyond. Death himself with all his angelic agents floated across the nation's screens in a phosphorescent haze of consolation. But with Ford, the emotional emphasis was not so much on the ultimate triumph and vindication of the dead as on the spiritual submission of the living to memory, tradition and even habit.

If *Judge Priest* represented Ford in a state of transition in 1934, *Steamboat 'Round the Bend* represented Ford in a state of fruition in 1935, but the film was completely lost amid the highbrow hooplah over *The Informer*, released a few months earlier. Sadly, it was Rogers' swan song as a performer, his death having preceded the release of this, his last film. Sadly, among many other reasons,

55

because Ford and Rogers had finally attained a marvellous rapport between their respective styles, thus achieving a mature exuberance that is virtually unique in the American cinema. Indeed, *Steamboat 'Round the Bend* is Ford's conveyance movie *par excellence*, even more than *Stagecoach* or *Wagonmaster*. The steamboat, after all, with all its gusto and energy and puffed up egoism must still submit to that most richly symbolic of all American rivers of life, the Mississippi, and both Ford and Rogers are alive equally to the exhilarating promise of the steamboat and to the sobering relentlessness of the river. Rogers is assisted ably by Anne Shirley, one of the more talented of the self-mockingly innocent ingénues of the Thirties; by Eugene Pallette, a roundly buoyant figure of a sheriff; and by Berton Churchill, a Ford regular as a villain but here more interestingly cast as a religious fanatic with a hatred of hard liquor. If the word Americana had not been squandered on so many trivial movies, it could be invoked this once and this once only for the spectacle of the climactic steamboat race in the course of which almost everything on board is sacrificed to the flames of competition.

There was a period in the late Forties when *Steamboat 'Round the Bend* and *Judge Priest* were reissued widely as a Will Rogers comedy double bill, but by this time there was a widespread reaction against the 'house-nigger' antics of Stepin' Fetchit, and the movies were pulled from distribution and never released to television. For his part, Ford unabashedly rehired Fetchit as late as 1953 for *The Sun Shines Bright*. Tradition or stagnation? It is certainly a very complex question. Ford, like Griffith, was nothing if not repentant towards the groups which had been victimized by the various American bigotries, but repentance for past sins is hardly the same thing as repudiation of past history. Of course, if it is easier for the old to repent than to repudiate, it is easier for the young to repudiate the past than to make an effort to understand it. But even among older liberals and radicals and egalitarians, the spectacle of Stepin' Fetchit mocking the unrelieved hypocrisy of American race relations must be painful indeed. Better that Fetchit be permanently unemployed than that he serve as a reminder of a shameful blind spot on both sides of the Mason–Dixon line. But for Ford, Mr Fetchit was an old friend and a familiar face, and he had to make a living like everyone else.

The issue for the film historian is more pointed still. Should we suppress the evidence of national bigotry in the past for the sake of the future? Aside from any commitment to the integrity of film scholarship, one could argue that the horrors of the past might serve to modify a paralysing disenchantment with the present. It is precisely because the past is too often glossed over as painless nostalgia that the present tends to become unendurable. Even this Ford enthusiast must testify that he winces when Stepin' Fetchit enacts the mock-castration of his race. The guilt and shame are almost too much to bear, but they are more appropriate feelings for members of America's master race than the smug self-satisfaction which would ensue from the high-minded suppression of Stepin' Fetchit.

To backtrack a year or so from *Steamboat 'Round the Bend*, we must turn to *The Lost Patrol* as another critical turning point in Ford's career. This was the first time that Ford and Nichols were associated on a project at RKO, and it marks the beginning of a studio dialectic in discussions of Ford's career. The influence of studio policies on Hollywood movies is more complex and less precisely measurable than most studio historians care to admit. After all, the same studio could and did sponsor John Barrymore and Rin-Tin-Tin, or Greta Garbo and Wallace Beery, or *Citizen Kane* and Hopalong Cassidy. Even in the Thirties and Forties when studio *esprit de corps* was at least more conspicuous than at other times, one's first impression of a studio is often considerably at variance with one's later research in depth.

Modern studio historians are not always too finicky about the once separate corporate strands (20th Century and Fox, Warners and First National), which have since been woven together for archival convenience. In Ford's case, it was actually during the shooting of *Steamboat 'Round the Bend* that the old-fashioned Fox studio founded by William Fox merged with 20th Century Pictures, the new-fangled company operated by Darryl F. Zanuck. For most of the Thirties, Fox, with or without the Zanuck accretion, was Ford's home studio, his bread and butter base, the place where he could compromise to his heart's content, or so his legend went. By contrast, RKO was the studio of his conscience, of his artistic aspiration, of his moral commitment to his material. And the RKO part of the legend actually began with *The Lost Patrol*, a saga of a

British cavalry patrol lost in the Mesopotamian desert, and being picked off at dramatic intervals by unseen Arabs until in the end only Victor McLaglen's Sergeant is left to tell the tale. But he remains mute when questioned by an officer in charge of a relief column, and just stares helplessly at the glistening swords marking the graves of his fallen comrades under the desert sun.

The Lost Patrol has been deflated over the years for its Gaelically garrulous heroics and for the excessive theatrics of some of the performers, especially Boris Karloff's religious fanatic. More important, the original context of the film has been lost irretrievably. The fact remains that *The Lost Patrol* was a legendary film in its own time and in the following decade when it was revived at action theatres in big cities. The late and very perceptive sports columnist Jimmy Cannon once cited *The Lost Patrol* as his favourite war film.

Modern film scholars fail to appreciate the comparative austerity of *The Lost Patrol* with respect to other works in the same period and genre. The irony implicit in men being killed by an unseen enemy gives the film a mystical quality. Here we have a fusion of the morbid pessimism of Dudley Nichols and the poetic meditation of John Ford's *mise en scène*. A large portion of the plot is concerned with the futile efforts of the men to catch even a fleeting glimpse of their enemy. As the frustrated victims stare into the void of the desert, they are grouped by Ford into a cluster of truth-seekers, into a parish of failed perceptions.

Jean Renoir has observed that all great art is ultimately abstract, an observation which may give us more of an insight into Renoir's art than into art itself. Here again, Ford resembles Renoir in that we recognize recurring poetic images in widely differing contexts. And no director in the history of the cinema has equalled Ford in poetically projecting the spectacle of man gazing out from his sanctuary at the perils of a distant destiny. That is why mere plot synopses are so misleading in the understanding of Ford's films. His art comes to life most vibrantly at the very moment when the plot pauses or even stops entirely. And it is in this sense that Ford's style so often transcends his scenarios.

However, it was necessary for Ford to tackle serious, ambitious projects for his style to be perceived at all. Hence, the crucial significance of the Ford–Nichols collaboration. Just as with *Men Without Women* at the beginning of the sound era, *The Lost Patrol* and *The Informer* provided Ford with an individuality without which he could never have received any substantial critical recognition. Even so, one can see in *The Lost Patrol* those elements with which Ford is most congenial, and those with which he is most uncomfortable. The religious fanatic, for example, is regarded with little of the obsessive subjectivity one might anticipate as a matter of course from Tod Browning or Georges Franju, not to mention such classical masters of morbidity as Murnau and Dreyer. Ford has no patience with monsters or ideologues – they are too abstracted and asocial for his taste. Ford's religion, like his patriotism, is essentially communal rather than ideological. Action audiences laugh uproariously at the spectacle of Karloff climbing the sand dune to implant a cross on its crest. At least some of the laughter is generated by the detachment with which Ford's camera views this allegorical ascent. By contrast, Gypo Nolan's entrance into the church at the confessional climax of *The Informer* is treated with hulking subjectivity so that the audience itself can partake of emotional absolution through Gypo's confession.

Lindsay Anderson has criticized Ford's subjective treatment of the church scene in *The Informer* for muddling the moral issues and vulgarizing the character with excessive focal magnification. It is partly a question of the actors in the two roles: Ford has no feeling for Karloff's wormy persona. Victor McLaglen, on the other hand, is virtually a Ford creation. Indeed, his performance in *The Lost Patrol* is in some respects even more spectacular than his more famous one in *The Informer*. There are few moments in the cinema as exhilarating as the one in which McLaglen, now the last survivor of his platoon, explodes with convulsive laughter to the rhythm of his machine-gun as he mows down the handful of Arabs who have for so long made life hell for him and his men. It is a moment of orgasmic release through violence that even Peckinpah has not approached in emotional intensity. And in 1934, and even in 1944, the screen was not yet so saturated with Peckinpowism that such a spine-tingling sequence could be dismissed lightly or forgotten quickly.

The rest of the acting ranges from the serviceable performances of Wallace Ford (also in *The Informer*) and Reginald Denny (as the familiar doomed English aristocrat in the Ford–Nichols mythos), to routine caricatures of national types – Cockney, Irish, Jewish, etc. – down to a ridiculously stiff-upper-lippish English flier who gets

61

The Lost Patrol: detachment; and a collective point of view

guffaws with his stock-ceremonial-simpering of 'I say there' as the Arabs splatter him with bullets. This reflects one of Ford's most parochial blind spots: he finds it hard to take the English very seriously. But flaws and rough edges aside, *The Lost Patrol* remains a memorable experience in the cinema. The acting and the reading of lines may not be all they should be, but the majestic implications of the spectacle cannot easily be ignored. Even when Ford falters on the dramatic and psychological aspects of his material, his epic instinct comes to the rescue. The collective signification of the figures in long shot redeems the deficiencies of the characters in close-up.

Lindsay Anderson was perhaps the first critic to turn the Ford–Nichols legend upside down by expressing a clear preference for Ford minus Nichols over Ford plus Nichols. In his reappraisal of Ford's career, Anderson went so far as to downgrade *The Lost Patrol* and *The Informer* even in terms of Max Steiner's 'blatant, imitative music'. In a footnote to this derogatory judgment, Anderson amplifies his disenchantment with the background music: 'Steiner's misguided contributions to both *The Lost Patrol* and *The Informer* were acutely characterized by the French composer, Maurice Jaubert, himself responsible for such masterly scores as those for *Zéro de Conduite* and *L'Atalante*, and for the pre-war films of Carné: "In *The Lost Patrol* – otherwise an admirable film – the director was apparently alarmed by the silence of the desert in which the story was laid. He might well have realized the dramatic possibilities of silence, but instead he assaulted the ear, without a moment's pause, with a gratuitous orchestral accompaniment which nearly destroyed the reality of the images. Another attitude was well illustrated in *The Informer*, where music was used to imitate the noise of coins falling, and even the gurgling of beer in a man's throat. This is not merely puerile, but a misconception of what music is . . ." (*World Film News*, July, 1936).'

The Steiner tendency towards musical mimesis was described by Oscar Levant as Mickey-Mousing, but Levant none the less championed such early Thirties RKO-Steiner scores as those for *The Most Dangerous Game, King Kong, Of Human Bondage* and *The Lost Patrol*. Steiner was an exotic figure in this period because background music without a natural source (i.e. radio, phonograph, visible musicians) had virtually disappeared from the Hollywood screen. Dialogue scenes, especially, were done *a capella*, partly in the name of realism, and partly in unconscious homage to the theatre. An ultra-modern film aesthetician like Jean-Luc Godard has expressed a sensuous delight in the unadorned sound of the human voice crackling on the crude soundtracks of the early talkies. And there has always been in highbrow film theory some sort of vague commitment to arty ellipsis and asynchronous counterpoint in the fusion of sound, speech and music with images. Hence, it always sounds reasonable to suggest that there should be less music or less dialogue in a given motion picture.

In Steiner's case, it is impossible to generalize from any one of his scores. *King Kong* is inconceivable without its Steiner score, but it is more a mood score in the manner of Alfred Newman than a Mickey Mouse score. Leslie Howard's limp in *Of Human Bondage* and the blind man's fateful cane-strokes in *The Informer* are augmented musically by Steiner not so much through sentimental vulgarity as through a desire of the period to amplify the impressions of the mind. This is the period, after all, in which Hitchcock was experimenting with images of purely mental montage (the roast chicken in *Murder*, the imaginary train in *The Man Who Knew Too Much*) and in which Mamoulian superimposed the kicking legs of Miriam Hopkins on the skull of Fredric March in *Dr Jekyll and Mr Hyde*. Steiner stood out in this period because his scores tended to define the mood of a film in a manner more tingly than the tinkly French could appreciate at the time. One can criticize Steiner more aptly much later for his too insistently heroic score for John Huston's sourish *The Treasure of the Sierra Madre*. Back in 1934 and 1935, however, Steiner was an inseparable part of the Ford–Nichols–RKO mystique, just as Gregg Toland was so often the key to the so-called quality look of Goldwyn films.

Although it was due to the success of *The Lost Patrol* that Ford was later granted the opportunity to make *The Informer*, he returned home to the Fox studio in the interim to make one of his worst movies, *The World Moves On*, a painfully transparent attempt by the studio to cash in on the previous year's success with the Frank Lloyd–Noël Coward *Cavalcade*. Reginald C. Berkeley's script for *The World Moves On* was talky, preachy and pompous, and Ford seemed to have little affinity as a director with either Madeleine Carroll or Franchot Tone, two of the more attractive ornaments of the Thirties – but for other directors.

The World Moves On is probably the picture which features in Ford's cryptic anecdote about a producer asking him to shoot the script exactly as it was written, and his complying with a vengeance so that the film ran way over length. But although Ford has little sympathy with the sprawling, multi-generational narrative of the film, in which the same players are reincarnated every half century or so, it must be noted on a thematic level that *The World Moves On* is one of many movies from the Thirties with an overtly anti-war message. In a sense, however, the social consciousness stirring at Fox through this period was as responsible for bad Ford movies like *The World Moves On* and the anti-gun-merchant-of-death *Four Men and a Prayer* as for such good Ford movies as *The Prisoner of Shark Island* and *The Grapes of Wrath*. Certainly, in terms of pure message, *The World Moves On* is more useful and venturesome than *The Lost Patrol* or *Stagecoach*, which indicates the often divergent paths of art and politics in the cinema.

Some of the war footage from *The World Moves On* was later used by Howard Hawks in *The Road to Glory*. Such borrowings were relatively common in the Thirties, particularly within the same studio, but the fact remains that *The Road to Glory* is far more effective and engrossing a movie than *The World Moves On*. One might say that Ford's flair for spectacle here found its dramatic context in a Hawks film.

The Whole Town's Talking is one of the most likable and least likely works in Ford's oeuvre. Its subject (gangster parody) and scriptwriter (Robert Riskin) and studio (Columbia) mark it even in retrospect as a more logical assignment for Frank Capra. Ford handles the material somewhat more broadly than Capra might have done; that is, more as a tall story than as a folksy vignette. But it is interesting that Ford is fully sensitive to the spunky working girl beauty and vitality of Jean Arthur a year before Capra made her one of the shining icons of the Thirties in *Mr Deeds Goes to Town*. Of course, Ford doesn't go ga-ga over Arthur with any of Capra's lyrical close-ups. Ford keeps his distance so that the comic narrative can flow freely, whereas Capra delights in those privileged moments when characters are suspended in the hushed close-ups of their innermost feelings.

The Whole Town's Talking reflected a tendency around the mid-

Thirties to burlesque the *film noir*, the most extreme example being the incredibly slapdash, slapstick version of *The Maltese Falcon* released at Warners under the title *Satan Met a Lady*. As a character star of the Thirties, Edward G. Robinson seemed especially eager to let the civilized side of his screen persona poke fun at its brutish side. In a poll of fan-magazine readers on the Warners gangster leads of the Thirties and early Forties, Jimmy Cagney was considered the toughest, Humphrey Bogart the meanest, George Raft the most sinister, and Edward G. Robinson the most lovable. Here Robinson was given a dual role through which his Walter Mitty side finally triumphed over his Little Caesar side. This Jekyll–Hyde form of cinematographic trickery was used quite often in the Thirties and Forties as a fairly elementary exercise in the art of acting out contrasting parts within the same visual frame. This device generally served either as a naïve mechanism of Manichean moralizing in which absolute good wrestled with absolute evil on identical facial landscapes, or as regenerative romance (particularly in such Ronald Colman vehicles as *The Masquerader* and *The Prisoner of Zenda*). In *The Dark Mirror*, Olivia De Havilland scored a double coup with this kind of visual duality by aligning good and bad sisters with her own good and bad profiles. But *The Whole Town's Talking* was by far the funniest of these double-headed enterprises, and also the most fascinating in reflecting the double thrust of Robinson's career from the mythic malignancy of *Little Caesar* to the sensitivity and humanity of his more civilized incarnations. There were funny performances also by Donald Meek, Ed Brophy and Wallace Ford, all of whom were to figure prominently in later Ford films.

Bob Thomas tells a fascinating story (in *King Cohn*) about Ford's eating in the Columbia commissary when the late Harry Cohn was bullying all the producers and directors to bet him on American football games. As the story goes, Ford pretended a complete ignorance of football, and thus conned Cohn into giving him an edge on the official point spread. What Cohn did not know was that Ford, far from being a native Irish soccer enthusiast as he had intimated, had actually played football at the University of Maine under the nickname of Bull Feeney. The anecdote is interesting not so much for its explicit content as for its suggestion of the devious behaviour of directors with studio executives in this era. Strangely, Ford seemed to get along unusually well with the much-maligned Cohn, and

Little Caesar and Walter Mitty: Edward G. Robinson (with Jean Arthur) in *The Whole Town's Talking*

returned to the Columbia studios on several occasions for some of his most rewarding projects. *The Whole Town's Talking* was a massive triumph for Edward G. Robinson, and a modest success for John Ford on the eve of *The Informer*, the one film, more than any other, which was to establish his reputation in Hollywood and the world.

The extraordinary critical acclaim accorded to *The Informer* in its time can be understood at least partly as a form of aesthetic amnesia. It is hard to believe in the 1970s that there was ever a time in the 1930s when *The Informer* could be regarded as the first 'creative'

American sound film. Few reviewers in 1935 seemed to recall such early Thirties sound classics as Sternberg's *The Blue Angel* and *Morocco*, Ernst Lubitsch's *Trouble in Paradise*, and Howard Hawks' *Scarface*. What had been forgotten most of all was the tradition of German Expressionism which had peaked in 1927 with Murnau's sublime *Sunrise*. Hence, Ford's moving camera, ghostly shadows, tinkling symbols and fog-shrouded studio backdrops struck many reviewers in 1935 as spectacularly 'cinematic' after years of talk, talk, talk on the sunny screens of theatrical adaptations. And six years later reviewers were to hail *Citizen Kane* for the same kind of gloom-and-doom innovations credited to *The Informer*, and again as if the German stylists of the Twenties had never existed. Ironically, anti-Expressionist critics and scholars like Otis Ferguson, James Agee and Richard Griffith were later to attack both *The Informer* and *Citizen Kane* for their alleged artiness and thematic superficiality.

However, *The Informer* did not become an instant classic simply for its formal style, but rather because its style was thought to be fused with a worthy theme. The fact that Gypo Nolan was a lower-class character with an empty belly was virtually sufficient in itself to make him a worthy protagonist of the Depression era. Meyer Levin, an extremely committed critic for *Esquire* in this period, made a special point of aligning himself with the grubby economic motivations for Gypo Nolan's Judas act in *The Informer* against the Gidean gratuitousness of the evil deeds performed by Noël Coward's upper-crust publisher in *The Scoundrel*, supposedly the last word in 1935 New York ultra-sophistication. Oddly enough, it is *The Scoundrel* rather than *The Informer* which degenerates into the ultimate silliness of spiritual redemption in the after-life by the shedding of a woman's tear to the strains not of a Max Steiner score, but of Rachmaninov's Second Piano Concerto, which later resounded on the soundtracks of *The Seventh Veil* (1945) and *Brief Encounter* (1946). Hence, what strikes critics of the Seventies as excessive sentimentality in *The Informer* was not nearly so unusual in the relatively soft-hearted Thirties.

None the less, *The Informer* remains one of the most disappointing of all official film classics in that its allegorical parallel with the Passion Play leads it away from pulsating drama into pious dogma. The biggest problem is with the character of Gypo Nolan, a pitiful giant doomed from the start to an endless night of need, shame, guilt, fear, and the most maudlin, drunken self-deception. With virtually the entire film devoted to his slow degradation and destruction, he remains helplessly muddled and inarticulate until Mother Church provides a false catharsis through Nolan's true confession to Una O'Connor's Mother Machreeish Mrs McPhillip, not so much a real mother in mourning for her son as a ritualized figurine of forgiveness for her son's betrayer.

What makes *The Informer* particularly uncomfortable is Gypo's pathetic yearning to rejoin the ultra-Fordian community – the IRA – which has been mobilized to destroy him. By sentimentalizing Preston Foster's IRA leader in the movie into a moony patriot, Ford and Nichols sacrifice Liam O'Flaherty's ambivalent treatment of the revolutionary as a dedicated Communist, and hence as cold-bloodedly cerebral in his way as Gypo is hot-bloodedly visceral in his. O'Flaherty is also less misty-eyed towards the women in his story than Ford is to both Margot Grahame's Magdalene and to Heather Angel's Madonna.

Even the most meticulous Ford scholars seem unfamiliar with a previous version of *The Informer*, a 1929 English silent film directed by German director Arthur Robison (*Warning Shadows, Manon Lescaut*) with Lars Hanson as Gypo Nolan and the German siren Lya de Putti (*Variety*) in the lead role as Katie Fox. In this instance, Ford's direction owes nothing to the earlier work, which, curiously, is less cluttered with foggy atmosphere and more modern-looking in its street ambience than the dreamy 'Danny Boy' Dublin on the RKO back lot. (As an added footnote to film history, *The Lost Patrol* had also been made previously with Victor McLaglen's brother, Cyril, in the part of the surviving sergeant.)

There are other striking differences between the two versions of *The Informer*. Lars Hanson's Gypo Nolan is a matinee idol next to Victor McLaglen's hulking brute, and the motivations differ accordingly. Whereas McLaglen's betrayal of his best friend is triggered by a gnawing hunger for money (twenty pounds equalling thirty pieces of silver), Hanson's betrayal is connected with a complicated sexual intrigue in which a contrived misunderstanding plays a large part. There is a great deal more gunplay and inconclusive chasing around in the Robison whereas the Ford is very tightly structured round the implacability of its allegory. But with the Robison also there is more of the paranoia of modern politics and less of Ford's Irish-Catholic Passion Play. Robison's revolutionary organization is a Party with all its attendant factional infighting; Ford's revolutionary organization is an Army with its attendant pomp and panoply, discipline and tradition. The Robison film is more sordid, the Ford more turgid. The Robison is more ambiguous, the Ford more lucid. Neither version is entirely faithful to the single literary source which they share, the Robison dragging in an unconvincing love interest, and the Ford sentimentally softening many of the cynical cross-purposes of the characters.

Still, what is most interesting about these two films is the extent to which they reflect the cataclysmic changes in the world and in the cinema between 1929 and 1935. For one thing, there is no intimation of worldwide poverty in the earlier version of *The Informer*. Unrest yes, but Depression no. By contrast, the Ford seems drenched with the damp despair of persistent hunger and unemployment. Ford's Dublin is a city of soup kitchens whereas Robison's is a city of dance halls. More important, Ford establishes a dialectical distinction between the thirty pieces of silver (coins tinkling symbolically on Steiner's soundtrack and shining with all the allegorical glow at the command of Joseph H. August's camera) and the twenty pounds (representing, in turn, conscience money to a blind man, dream money of a trip to America first-class, shame money to the dead man's family, love money to a whore, food and drink money for an orgy of fish-and-chips and a Walpurgisnacht of Irish dialect humour). If the thirty pieces of silver look forward to *The Fugitive*, the twenty pounds of currency negotiable in the things of this world look forward to the class yearnings of *The Grapes of Wrath* and *How Green Was My Valley*. All in all, *The Informer* never overcomes the handicap of its sub-Aristotelian protagonist and its excessively pious sentimentality. But it is a film symptomatic of its time, and its stunning transformation of Margot Grahame from a Madonna to a Magdalene, simply by having her remove her shawl to reveal a perky hat, is one of the most privileged moments in all cinema, achieving with *mise en scène* what Vivien Leigh achieved with sheer beauty in *Waterloo Bridge* five years later.

Ford made three films in 1936 – *The Prisoner of Shark Island* for 20th Century-Fox, and *Mary of Scotland* and *The Plough and the*

The Informer: the price of betrayal (Victor McLaglen)

Stars for RKO. And within this one year the Ford–Nichols–RKO mystique completely collapsed, and a new theory was born to provide a collective rationale for Ford's rising career. It was the 20th Century-Fox–Darryl F. Zanuck–Nunnally Johnson–Kenneth MacGowan–Lamarr Trotti–Phillip Dunne theory to take us from *The Prisoner of Shark Island* through *Young Mr Lincoln, The Grapes of Wrath* and *How Green Was My Valley*. Along the way there were all sorts of bumps and detours like *Wee Willie Winkie, Four Men and a Prayer, Submarine Patrol, Drums Along the Mohawk* and *Tobacco Road*, or so it seemed to informed observers at the time and after. It was as if John Ford's directorial soul were the arena for a titanic struggle between the romantic artifices of Dudley Nichols and the realist humanism of the Fox contingent. What was actually happening was that Ford's art was becoming richer and more complex as he played off one aesthetic against another. He was not yet fully in command of his career, but he was discovering his true talents and affinities through productive experience rather than through effete predisposition. He was sifting the tasks from the pleasures, and, in the process, learning to tell all sorts of stories, the taller and fancier the better, with the utmost efficiency and dispatch. Hence, even his failures of this period help us to understand his later masterpieces.

The Prisoner of Shark Island (one of the most satisfying of Ford's Thirties films) begins with a series of ceremonial vignettes culminating in the assassination of Abraham Lincoln, America's own Passion

71

Play. The waxworks portrayal of Lincoln by Frank McGlynn, Snr., is in the traditional mould, but Ford does something special with this memorial figure who embodies both the homely and the heroic, the immediate and the immortal. In death Ford's Lincoln comes to rest in the slowly fading tapestry of legend, not with the sense of a personal destiny as in D. W. Griffith's and Walter Huston's Lincoln, but rather with the gentle implacability of submission to the needs of a nation.

The focus then shifts to the trials and tribulations of Dr Samuel A. Mudd, a true-life victim of the miscarriages of justice which followed the Lincoln assassination. This is the year of *Fury* (inspired by a lynching in California), *Winterset* (inspired by the Sacco–Vanzetti case and its imagined aftermath) and of *Mr Deeds Goes to Town*. It is the year before *The Life of Emile Zola* with the Dreyfus case as its dramatic climax. Of course, audiences had to be assured in each instance that the victim was absolutely innocent of all the charges against him. It was never argued too strenuously that all men must be presumed innocent until proven guilty, and that it was far better for a hundred guilty persons to escape punishment than for one innocent person to be punished unjustly. Quite the contrary. Many movies openly encouraged mob vengeance and vigilante tactics even as other movies sobbed over condemned innocents with whom audiences could lovingly identify. *The Prisoner of Shark Island* depends therefore on a dangerously sentimental plot premise when it suggests that people like us should not be locked up with people like them.

The condescending us–them (as opposed to the ennobling I–thou) dichotomy is nowhere more bothersome than in Mudd's imperious attitude to the cowardly black soldiers temporarily terrorized by the plague on Shark Island until Mudd's threats with a slave-owning Southern accent terrorize them even more. We are just a few steps removed here in 1936 from the general historical assumptions promulgated in 1915 by D. W. Griffith in *Birth of a Nation*. Hence, aside from Father Abraham, the North was a pestilential horde of scalawags and carpetbaggers visited upon the prostrate but still civilized Southland. The most disruptive act of all was the North's granting of guns and votes to the dear darkies, thus alienating them from their loving masters and mistresses, most notably Margaret Sullavan in the King Vidor–Stark Young *So Red the Rose* and Vivien Leigh in *Gone With the Wind*. Still, the blacks are somewhat less degraded in *The Prisoner of Shark Island* and *So Red the Rose* than in most other films of the time. If they are not yet irrevocably rebellious, they are at least poised on the brink of manly defiance. That they are not so much separatist as surly betokens the desperately limited options of the black in the cinema of the Thirties, even under the most liberal auspices.

None the less, Ford stages the violent confrontations in *The Prisoner of Shark Island* for everything they are worth. The black mutiny, especially, is photographed with a towering monumentality which somehow evokes both Eisenstein and Dumas, that is, both the phallic thrust of revolutionary history and the subjective vertigo of Gothic romance. Yet the most idiosyncratically Fordian images remain those of submission, redemption and communion – Warner Baxter's Dr Samuel A. Mudd vindicating himself not through escape or revenge, but through service to his sworn enemies; John Carradine's sadistic jailer demanding to be the first to sign Mudd's petition for a pardon; and, most memorably Fordian of all, the return home of Mudd and his black neighbour (Ernest Whitman) to their respective families, each with their separate reunions within the one communal frame of the family of mankind. That the black family of Buckland Montmorency 'Buck' Tilford is conspicuously numerous next to the Mudd clan may be regarded as a racial cliché in the abstract, but not in the particularity of Ford's loving gaze.

Mary of Scotland brought Ford into contact for the first and last time with Katharine Hepburn's radiantly brash beauty, Maxwell Anderson's pedestrian blank verse, and Fredric March's practised hamminess in period roles. Most of all, it brought Ford face to face with his own deepest religious and ethnic prejudices: a woman named Mary, in history something of a Magdalene, but with the aid of Joseph August's camera filters, Ford's pure and sweet Madonna armed with her acceptance of herself as a woman against Elizabeth's monstrously repressed English Protestant spinster. I have triumphed over you as a woman, Mary declares on her way to the executioner's block. My son shall be king. Not I have loved, but my son shall be king. King of England or Crown Prince of Paradise, one madonna's pride is very much like another's. And with Katharine Hepburn cast as Mary and Florence Eldridge (Mrs Fredric March) as Elizabeth, the dramatic one-sidedness of this historical pageant becomes oppressive.

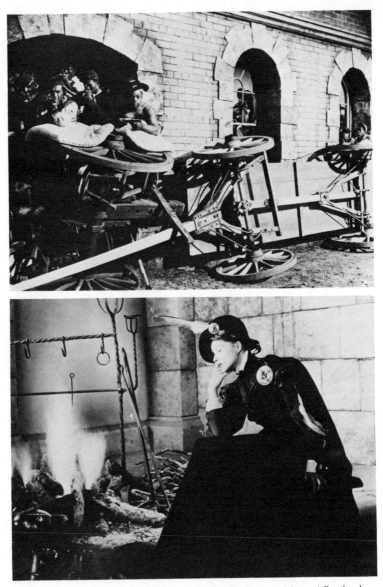

The Prisoner of Shark Island; (*below*) Katharine Hepburn as *Mary of Scotland*

74

Ford's technique here is expert enough, but his sensibility seems unduly primitive in this particular context. John Carradine's ill-fated Italianate fop David Rizzio becomes the first of a strange series of histrionic figures in the Ford community, figures for whom Ford begins by asking only a bemused tolerance, but with whom he ends up identifying in a curiously furtive way, as if the gruff man's mask Ford always affected in Hollywood concealed beneath it certain delicate, feminized features of the tenderest sensibility. The ham actor played by Alan Mowbray in *My Darling Clementine* and *Wagonmaster* is perhaps the ultimate expansion of John Carradine's, David Rizzio. Otherwise, *Mary of Scotland*, like *The Informer*, suffers from a form of sentimental masochism endemic in the Twenties and Thirties, decades in which paranoia was acted out literally and laboriously as interminable persecution.

For all its shortcomings, however, *Mary of Scotland* was at least a coherent film, whereas *The Plough and the Stars* that same year from the same studio emerged as ill-edited excerpts from at least three different movies. One of these movies involves the excruciating nagging of Barbara Stanwyck's Nora Clitheroe in her unsuccessful effort to keep Preston Foster's Jack Clitheroe from joining the Irish Rebellion in Easter Week, 1916. The second movie was adapted piecemeal by Dudley Nichols from Sean O'Casey's disenchanted bar-room drama of Irish character set against the ironic background of the Rebellion, and featured many of the original Abbey Players – Barry Fitzgerald, Dennis O'Dea, Eileen Crowe, Arthur Shields and F. J. McCormick (the last named especially memorable eleven years later in *Odd Man Out*, and so cited in Harold Pinter's Seventies play of absurdist reminiscence, *Old Times*). Then there was a third movie, on the Irish Rebellion itself: stirring, heroic, disastrous in Ford's most Homeric manner.

Unfortunately, the Stanwyck movie, the O'Casey movie and the Ford movie work at cross-purposes from one sequence to the next. Until recently, the weight of critical opprobrium fell most heavily upon Stanwyck for exemplifying the frivolous Hollywood star ethos to the detriment of the more serious concerns of O'Casey (poetic) and Ford (epic). The Girl, the Love Interest, the Soupçon of Sex: these were once supposed to be the shameful compromises Hollywood imposed upon artists (all male) like Ford and Nichols and O'Casey. Critics of the Seventies are more likely to criticize

Ford for misusing Stanwyck in view of her electrifying performances for Frank Capra (*The Miracle Woman*), King Vidor (*Stella Dallas*), Howard Hawks (*Ball of Fire*), Preston Sturges (*The Lady Eve*), Billy Wilder (*Double Indemnity*) and Samuel Fuller (*Forty Guns*). Let us say simply that the most thankless role for an actress is that of the wife or sweetheart who pleads with the hero not to engage in a violent, dangerous action for which the audience is yearning. It is an especially thankless role for an emotionally decisive actress like Stanwyck. All in all, she was much too much her own woman to submit meekly to the imperatives of a man's world, but without a meaningful context her performance degenerated into whining and wailing.

Ford's commitment to Sean O'Casey was confirmed in 1965 with *Young Cassidy*, a film Ford prepared but was too ill to direct, based on the autobiographical *Mirror in My House* by O'Casey, and finally directed by Jack Cardiff. Ford seems more indulgent to the Irish vices of drinking and fantasizing than does O'Casey, and too often the dramatist's glower is softened by the director's glow. But it has always been the nature of the film medium to enhance the romantic and the heroic at the expense of the sardonic and the ironic. Hence, Alfred Hitchcock's otherwise literal transcription of O'Casey's *Juno and the Paycock* ends with the glory of Juno mourning her dead son, whereas the original play ends with the grubbiness of the Paycock mumbling foolishly in his cups.

Wee Willie Winkie remains the most notorious assignment of John Ford's career in that as a supposed man's man he was called upon to direct that coyest of Hollywood childcult nymphets, Shirley Temple; and that as the supposed Irish patriot of *The Informer* and *The Plough and the Stars* he was compelled to perpetuate Hollywood's glorification of C. Aubrey Smith's British Empire, shifting from Liam O'Flaherty and Sean O'Casey to Rudyard Kipling. As the sweetest army brat in creation, Miss Temple seems in retrospect to have been too much the performing prodigy ever to generate genuine emotional responses. She always seemed much older than her years, supremely confident, aloof and self-sufficient. She lacked the emotional energy of Jackie Cooper and Margaret O'Brien and Roddy McDowall or the bratty virtuosity of Mitzi Green and Jane Withers and Jackie Searl or the vulnerably premature beauty of

76

Wee Willie Winkie: the funeral procession

Freddy Bartholomew, Bobby Breen, Gloria Jean and Elizabeth Taylor. Still, she was the most popular child star in the history of motion pictures (if one excepts Mary Pickford's long career of counterfeit childhood), and as such she automatically provides sociological insights into mass tastes of the Thirties, and especially the period's susceptibility to authoritarian goody-goodness.

Curiously, however, the movie is not unpleasing, with its zestful retelling of storybook romance from a child's wide-eyed point of view through a fringed curtain very much like a coarse camera filter. Victor McLaglen provides the blustering emotional coefficient to Miss Temple's pretty *sang-froid*, and Ford seized upon a rainy day to improvise the shooting of a stirring funeral, much as he later shot into a storm to capture the realistically climatic tension of an army patrol on the move in *She Wore a Yellow Ribbon*. Thus, Ford once again demonstrates his profound resemblance to Renoir in his willingness to tinker with the sacred scenario for visual truth.

The Hurricane belongs at first glance to that interesting genre of natural disaster movies in which the Thirties abounded, and for which James Basevi was justly honoured for his special effects extraordinary. The fires flaming in *In Old Chicago*, the typhoon in *Suez*, the earthquake in *San Francisco*, the swarm of locusts in *The Good Earth*, and the hurricane here attested to a period passion for apocalyptic demons *ex machina* to resolve all the complications of

The Hurricane: Mary Astor, Raymond Massey

the plot. Certainly, few plots were more complicated than that of *The Hurricane*, adapted by Dudley Nichols and Oliver H. P. Garrett from the novel by Charles Nordhoff and James Norman Hall of *Mutiny on the Bounty* fame. Social significance, tribal tabu, allegorical archetype and novelistic nuance are all crowded together on a placid South Seas Island where a French Governor (Raymond Massey) observes the letter of the law in confining Terangi (Jon Hall) to prison. Terangi escapes again and again to rejoin his bride Marama, and each time (but the very last) he is recaptured and his sentence extended. On his last escape, Terangi kills his archtormentor among the prison guards (John Carradine), but is in effect pardoned for his crime against his oppressor by the native god of the volcano which destroys the island and most of its inhabitants.

Terangi and Marama (especially in the glossy pseudo-primitive incarnations of Jon Hall and Dorothy Lamour) possess none of the metaphysical stature of the passionate protagonists in F. W. Murnau's *Tabu*. Terangi and Marama are merely the innocent victims of imperialist presumption and rigidity. The film's dramatic focus shifts therefore to the Europeans, and particularly to one of the most fascinatingly civilized of all movie couples – Raymond Massey's Governor De Laage and Mary Astor's Mrs De Laage. *The Hurricane* is ultimately *their* story as they argue with exquisite delicacy and tact the conflicting claims of the law and the heart. (Curiously, Massey and Astor played a very similar couple at about the same time in the John Cromwell–David O. Selznick *The Prisoner of Zenda*.) C. Aubrey Smith's Father Paul and Thomas Mitchell's Dr. Kersaint provide respectively the sacred and secular resonance for the moral debate of the De Laages.

Unfortunately, the civilized subtlety of the Massey character seems to have been misremembered even in so accurate and authoritative a book as Peter Bogdanovich's *John Ford*, in which the Governor is described simply as 'sadistic'. Massey is closer to being a man for all seasons in that he insists on governing his passions with his principles. Also, he finally redeems himself with a deliberated act of mercy, and such redemption and deliberation is hardly the mark of a sadist. Ultimately, however, the essential worthiness of the Massey character is reflected most luminously in the searching eyes of Mary Astor's complex creation of a wife, the most completely satisfying woman in all the predominantly masculine cinema of John Ford, and hence almost an intruder upon his vision of the world. The Vera Miles character in *The Man Who Shot Liberty Valance*, the Joanne Dru character in *Wagonmaster* and the Maureen O'Hara character in *Wings of Eagles* are magnificent creations, but they tend more to emotional inscrutability characteristic of the forces of nature than to Mary Astor's single-track lucidity of mind and heart.

Only the most dedicated Ford scholars can find much of lasting interest in Ford's two projects for 1938 – *Four Men and a Prayer* and *Submarine Patrol*. A Barry Fitzgerald drunk scene here, a shipboard mood scene there, and tongue-in-cheek banality everywhere. The male lead in both films was Richard Greene, a dull predecessor of Richard Todd in the earnest leading man category. His co-star in *Four Men* was the indefatigable Loretta Young, coolly competent, ultra-professional, somewhat too precisely photogenic with no lasting mythic glow. Nancy Kelly, the shore-leave love interest in *Submarine Patrol*, achieved her first apotheosis as the nagging wife of Tyrone Power's (and Henry King's) *Jesse James*, and her second many years later as the fearful mother of Patty McCormack's malignant tot in *The Bad Seed*. Ford's direction in both films appeared sluggish and disconnected, though both scripts seemed thematically consistent with the communal concerns of his vision. Ford's career had apparently sunk into an irreversible decline.

The fact is, I am quite happy in a movie, even a bad movie. Other people, so I have read, treasure memorable moments in their lives – the time one climbed the Parthenon at sunrise, the summer night one met a lonely girl in Central Park and achieved with her a sweet and natural relationship, as they say in books. I, too, once met a girl in Central Park, but it is not much to remember. What I remember is the time John Wayne killed three men with a carbine as he was falling to the dusty street in *Stagecoach*, and the time the kitten found Orson Welles in the doorway in *The Third Man*.

Walker Percy, The Moviegoer

Among Hollywood historians, 1939 has always been considered a big year for movies, particularly after the widely denigrated off-year of 1938. Indeed, most knowledgeable diagnosticians of the production pulse have always dipped the graph lines of artistic quality at 1929, 1934 and 1938; 1929 because of the awkwardness of the transition to sound, 1934 because of the resurgence of puerile censorship, and 1938 because of a mysterious suspension of inspiration. However, revisionist film critics in search of neglected masterpieces have tended to flatten out the yearly graphs somewhat. After all, how inferior a year could 1938 have been if it yielded such vintage champagnes as George Cukor's *Holiday*, Howard Hawks' *Bringing Up Baby*, Frank Borzage's *Three Comrades* and Alfred Hitchcock's *Young and Innocent* and *The Lady Vanishes*.

Whether we take the revisionist line or not, 1939 movies were nothing if not ambitious. And not merely because it was the year of *Gone With the Wind*, that massive confection from the crowded kitchen and many cooks of David O. Selznick: two directors (George Cukor and Victor Fleming), a platoon of writers (all but Sidney Howard uncredited), a cast of thousands, and a gross of millions. There were also Frank Capra's *Mr Smith Goes to Washington*, Ernst Lubitsch's *Ninotchka*, Leo McCarey's *Love Affair*, George Cukor's

The Women, Mitchell Leisen's *Midnight*, Michael Curtiz's *Four Wives*, and King Vidor's *Northwest Passage*. There were movies that seemed more significant at the time than they did later – William Wyler's *Wuthering Heights* (winner of the New York Film Critics Award over both Oscar-sweeping *Gone With the Wind* and *Mr Smith Goes to Washington*), William Dieterle's *Juarez*, Anatole Litvak's *Confessions of a Nazi Spy*, and Sam Wood's *Goodbye, Mr Chips*. There were movies also that seemed less interesting at the time than they would seem later – Howard Hawks' *Only Angels Have Wings*, Alfred Hitchcock's *Jamaica Inn*, Raoul Walsh's *The Roaring Twenties*, Cecil B. DeMille's *Union Pacific* and John Stahl's *When Tomorrow Comes*. Then there were the kind of fun movies that are never taken seriously enough – George Stevens' *Gunga Din*, George Marshall's *Destry Rides Again*, Zoltan Korda's *Four Feathers*, Michael Powell's *The Spy in Black*, and Busby Berkeley's *Babes in Arms*. Yet with all this lively competition, the one directorial reputation that shone more brightly than any other in 1939 was that of John Ford for his direction of *Stagecoach* and, secondarily, *Young Mr Lincoln* and *Drums Along the Mohawk*, and this is one official verdict that has stood the test of time.

What is most interesting about *Stagecoach* is that it does not seem to be about anything by 1939 standards. Nor is it derived from a Great Work of Literature, except possibly by osmosis. 'I still like that picture,' Ford told Bogdanovich. 'It was really *Boule de suif*, and I imagine the writer, Ernie Haycox, got his idea from there and turned it into a Western story which he called *Stage to Lordsburg*.' Or as I wrote in the *New York Times* of 12 May, 1968: 'Dudley Nichols's script has received almost as much credit for *Stagecoach* as John Ford's direction, but the literary ghost hovering over the entire project is de Maupassant.'

None the less, the plot-line of *Stagecoach* is closer to such criss-crossing strangers-when-we-meet exercises as *Grand Hotel, Union Depot* and *Transatlantic* than to the bitter social ironies of *Boule de suif*. As Leslie Fiedler has observed, American folklore explicitly denies the feudal hangover of European class structures. For de Maupassant, the social chasm between Boule de suif and her bourgeois travelling companions can never be bridged by sentimental plot devices. By contrast, Claire Trevor's Dallas is fully redeemed from her career as a Magdalene by her Madonna-like sweetness with the new-born babe of a respectable woman. And at the end of the film, the two men who have despised her most have had their comeuppance – John Carradine's gentleman gambler with an Apache bullet in his heart, and Berton Churchill's absconding banker by being publicly unmasked and hauled off to the hoosegow.

Thus, whereas de Maupassant's story evolves as a bitterly ironic investigation and indictment of bourgeois hypocrisy, *Stagecoach* emerges as a Christian-populist morality play with its heart on its sleeve. It might be noted in passing that the historical heavies in the de Maupassant story are Bismarck's victorious Germans, and so the tone is cynically defeatist in the Old World manner. Not so in the New World. *Stagecoach* is the first of the Seventh Cavalry celebrations of the extermination of the American Indian, and Ford does not spare the horses in pounding out a dance of racial triumph and exultation. It must be remembered that audiences in 1939, particularly in the cities, were far from surfeited with the melodrama and mythology of the Indian savage on the warpath.

On the whole, the Western had not fared too well in the Thirties, and the epic Western least of all. *Cimarron*, in 1931, was less a celebration of Manifest Destiny than a liberal critique of materialist values in old Oklahoma. After the land rush, there was precious little spectacle, only tiresome domestic discord and rhetorical flailing of underdog causes. *Billy the Kid, Law and Order* and *The Plainsman* tended to resolve their problems more with six-shooters at claustrophobically close range than with rifles at scenically long range.

Thus *Stagecoach* was more the beginning than the summing up of a tradition, and when we think of the Seventh Cavalry riding to the rescue of white womanhood, we are thinking no further back than *Stagecoach*. It is what has followed *Stagecoach* that makes *Stagecoach* seem traditional today, but in its own time the Ford film was a stunning stylistic revelation. Why? First and foremost, it moved in the most obvious manner, and hence it was considered eminently cinematic. Today, it is surprising to discover how much of *Stagecoach* is conventionally theatrical (*Kane* ceilings and all) and expressionistically shadowy, and how little of it actually opens up to the great outdoors of Monument Valley, Ford's private preserve for the next quarter of a century. *Stagecoach* was not actually the first movie shot in Monument Valley. But Ford made it seem that way. As he explained the choice of locale to Bogdanovich,

'Expressionistically shadowy': *Stagecoach* (John Carradine, Louise Platt, George Bancroft)

'I knew about it. I had travelled up there once, driving through Arizona on my way to Santa Fe, New Mexico.'

It is hard to realize in the Seventies that moviegoers had never been consciously aware of Monument Valley on the screen before *Stagecoach*. Anyone who has followed Ford's career with any consistency since *Stagecoach* must respond to the landscape of Monument Valley as to the New York skyline; that is, as to a fixed landmark of our visual imagination. But with this difference: Monument Valley belongs to Ford and to Ford alone, and is thus not so much a locale or even a subject as a stylistic signature. And it belongs to Ford, not merely because of *Stagecoach*, but because Ford did not hesitate to use Monument Valley again and again to the occasional amusement and derision of those of his colleagues who are ever on the lookout for brand new locations.

The point is that *Stagecoach* has been clarified and validated by what has followed. Its durability as a classic is attributable not so much to what people thought about it at the time as to what Ford himself spun off from it in his subsequent career. Indeed, there was a time in the late Fifties and early Sixties when New Critics in various countries tended to write off Ford and *Stagecoach* as the ultimate expressions of an outworn classicism. The very perfection of *Stagecoach* was held against it. Movies were supposed to slop off round the edges with intimations of personal obsession.

A particularly damaging attitude towards *Stagecoach* was con-

'A stylistic signature': Monument Valley in *Stagecoach*

tained in the end-of-an-era comments of the late, great, but none the less mistaken André Bazin:

> In seeing again today such films as *Jezebel* by William Wyler, *Stagecoach* by John Ford, or *Le Jour se lève* by Marcel Carné, one has the feeling that in them an art has found its perfect balance, its ideal form of expression, and reciprocally one admires them for dramatic and moral themes to which the cinema, while it may not have created them, has given a grandeur, an artistic effectiveness, that they would not otherwise have had. In short, here are all the characteristics of the ripeness of a classical art.

Bazin's importance as a critic, and he *is* one of the most important aestheticians in the history of the cinema, lies in his persuasive challenge to the montage theories of Eisenstein and Pudovkin, theories which had reigned supreme not only among film aestheticians, but among producers who always believed that they could save anything in the cutting room. Ironically, Bazin discovered new culture heroes in the Wyler of *The Little Foxes* and the Welles of

Citizen Kane (both films photographed by Gregg Toland). Ironically because Welles himself studied *Stagecoach* assiduously before undertaking *Citizen Kane*. None the less, Bazin considered Welles and Wyler formally more advanced than Ford: 'The story-telling of Welles or Wyler is no less explicit than John Ford's but theirs has the advantage over his in that it does not sacrifice the specific effects that can be derived from unity of image in space and time.'

Thus, from a certain point of view, *Stagecoach* is a triumph of classical editing in the Thirties manner, and nothing more. Given the Nichols–Haycox–de Maupassant material, any director of the Thirties might have come up with *Stagecoach*, or so Bazin expects us to believe. However, with the benefit of more than three decades of hindsight, it is more apparent than ever before that *Stagecoach* could not have been made by anyone but Ford. What seemed once like a functional mechanism of entertainment now reverberates with an impressive array of Fordian themes and motifs – the redemption of the harlot (Claire Trevor), the regeneration of the drunkard (Thomas Mitchell), the revenge of the bereaved brother (John Wayne), the self-sacrifice of a self-condemned aristocrat (John Carradine), and the submergence of the group in the symbolic conveyance of a cause (the stagecoach itself). Above all, there is the sense of an assemblage of mythical archetypes outlined against the horizons of history, but not as the stiffly laundered statuary of Frank Lloyd's *Wells Fargo*, or the small-scale Leatherstockings of Cecil B. DeMille's *Union Pacific*. What makes Ford's characters unique in the Western Epic is their double image, alternating between close-ups of emotional intimacy and long shots of epic involvement, thus capturing both the twitches of life and the silhouettes of legend.

This, then, is the ultimate justification of Ford's classical editing: that it expresses as economically as possible the personal and social aspects of his characters. And it is this economy of expression that makes Ford one of the foremost poets of the screen. It can be argued that *Stagecoach*, even before *Citizen Kane*, anticipates the modern cinema's emphasis on personal style as an end in itself. And it can be argued also that, though Ford's style is less visible than Welles', it is eminently more visual, as Welles himself would generously admit.

Whereas *Stagecoach*, like *The Informer*, was overpublicized at the outset as an instant classic, *Young Mr Lincoln*, like *Judge Priest* and

Steamboat 'Round the Bend, has taken longer to become a legendary masterpiece in Ford's career. At the very least, *Young Mr Lincoln* is the airiest Ford film up to this time, and the most relaxed in the deceptively casual and carefree manner so reminiscent of Renoir's *La Règle du Jeu*. Ford's pacing had been leisurely enough in the past – *Just Pals* and the Will Rogers movies come immediately to mind for their slowpoke cinematics – but never before had he combined such slowness of narrative development with such intensity of emotional expression. The director was greatly aided by a promising young Fox contract player named Henry Fonda, with whose prairie populist features and shaggy dog vocalisms Ford was to be associated subsequently on *Drums Along the Mohawk, The Grapes of Wrath, My Darling Clementine, The Fugitive, Fort Apache*, and finally *Mr Roberts*, the stormy production which caused a rupture in their relationship.

It is hard to believe that Fonda was once the third-ranking Fox leading man behind Tyrone Power and Don Ameche, but such he was and such he might have remained had he and Ford not made film history together. Still, Fonda never achieved either the mythic magnitude of the personality movie stars like Cagney, Stewart, Grant, Wayne, Bogart, Cooper, Gable or the critical cachet accorded to the likes of Arliss, Muni, José Ferrer and other disguise artists for burying the personality in the part under a ton of make-up. Fonda's Young Lincoln was a case in point as an intermediate performance in 1939 between James Stewart's forceful projection of his own personality in *Mr Smith Goes to Washington* and Robert Donat's uncanny incarnation of old age in *Goodbye, Mr Chips*, an illustrious example of seemingly ageing from within.

Significantly, Stewart won the New York Film Critics Award that year, and Robert Donat the Oscar, but Fonda's performance fell by the wayside. Indeed, Raymond Massey was hailed the following year in the John Cromwell–Robert E. Sherwood *Abe Lincoln in Illinois* for so closely resembling the Great Emancipator visually, unlike Walter Huston's excessively idiosyncratic Lincoln for D. W. Griffith and Henry Fonda's for John Ford. As it was, Fonda's limited make-up (mostly around the nose) suggested Lincoln without subverting Fonda, so that over the years Fonda's performance has gained in stature as an actor's perceptive commentary on a legend.

The obsessive reincarnation of Lincoln in the American cinema through the Thirties and early Forties can be analysed from many different perspectives. On the most edifying level, Lincoln exemplified, as few American national heroes have done, the egalitarian illusions of the American people, specifically their log cabin syndrome with which the Griffith film begins and ends. Lincoln's Gettysburg Address still warms democratic hearts with its intimation of a commoner's brevity and simplicity prevailing in a public place over the rhetorical and metaphorical excesses of an elitist (Edward Everett). On the personal level, triumph commingles with tragedy. Lincoln preserved the Union and liberated the slaves, but at the cost of a Civil War. Death claimed his first love, Ann Rutledge; and dissension clouded his subsequent marriage to Mary Todd. But somehow Lincoln's marital troubles made him all the more the quintessential American hero and martyr. Indeed, a radio series in the Forties actually exploited the image of Lincoln as a henpecked husband in the Jiggs-and-Maggie tradition of the comic strip *Bringing Up Father. Young Mr Lincoln* opened in that very pivotal period when a World Depression was ending and a World War was beginning. Sacrifice and suffering were in the air, and it seemed fitting that the tragicomic muses of Frank Capra and Leo McCarey should be eclipsed by the more austerely tragic muse of John Ford.

Ford complained to Peter Bogdanovich that the studio cut out a short sequence in which young Lincoln encounters young John Wilkes Booth in front of a Springfield theatre in which the Booth family is performing *Hamlet.* What is most interesting about this production story is that there are clearly two sides to it. One can argue that it is a bit obvious and even pseudo-prophetic in the most lurid popular romance manner to force a confrontation between Lincoln and Booth so early in their ill-fated lives. It is as if Mrs Iscariot dropped in to the manger to see how little Jesus was doing, and began carrying on about her own son, Judas.

However, Ford had never been a director to shrink from the obvious, and surprisingly often he brings it off by the sheer strength and tenacity of his visual style. He is also a master of the telling detail *en passant,* so that the epic sweep of Lincoln's ride through the muddy streets of Springfield could just possibly reduce the forced encounter with Booth from an event to an incident. Or possibly not; we shall never know. Still, it is very characteristic of Ford not to make any effort to dissociate Lincoln from his fatal legend, but rather to affix the ultimate assassination on his yet unfurrowed brow like a halo. As it is, *Young Mr Lincoln* abounds (even without young Mr Booth) with intimations of immortality. Lincoln's playing on his Jew's harp of a 'new, catchy tune' we recognize as *Dixie*, Lincoln's first political speech in Springfield photographed with folksy intimacy, but given an other-worldly dimension of destiny by Alfred Newman's recurring musical theme, Ford's improvisational exploitation of a fortuitous storm to effect an elemental dissolve from the distant shot of a lanky man in a stovepipe hat on a storm-tossed hilltop to the granite grandeur of the Lincoln Memorial, which curiously figures also in the final inspirational frame of *Mr Smith Goes to Washington.*

Ford is capable also of symbolic ellipsis, particularly in his handling of Lincoln's shortlived romance with Ann Rutledge. Ford worked on the script with Lamarr Trotti, and thus managed to compress the romance into two lateral tracking shots, both from right to left, the first ending on a fence by the river in springtime, the second integrating the flow of an ice-strewn river with Lincoln's walk to the cemetery by the river where he resumes his conversation with Ann Rutledge by asking her gravestone whether he should move on to Springfield or stay behind in Kentucky. He flips a coin, and the next lateral movement we see is from left to right into Springfield. Conversations with the dead go back to the *Oresteia* and beyond, but the low-key matter-of-factness with which Fonda and Ford handle this scene makes it comparable in its evocation of eternity to the greatest moments in Mizoguchi.

The dramatic core of *Young Mr Lincoln* is a tumultuous trial in which two brothers are falsely accused of murder, and here Fonda's offbeat calm and delayed deadpan humour play to good effect against the assorted hysterics of Alice Brady's pioneer mother of the accused, Donald Meek's bumbling prosecutor, and Ward Bond's unmasked murderer. Alice Brady had passed from screwball society matrons earlier in the Thirties to emotionally convincing pioneer matriarchs in Henry King's *In Old Chicago* and *Young Mr Lincoln.* For his part, Donald Meek was so much a part of Ford's world as the little man with the perpetual quaver in his voice and the perpetual panic in his eyes that it seemed almost sadistic to send him up against Fonda's Lincoln in a Springfield courtroom, and especially the kind of boisterous courtroom Ford conducted out of his ill-concealed

Young Mr Lincoln: the walk by the river (Henry Fonda, Pauline Moore)

fondness for low humour and hammy theatrics. It is interesting to compare Bond's extremely histrionic breakdown away from the witness chair and on his guilt-ridden knees with a similar courtroom breakdown in *Sergeant Rutledge* more than two decades later. In both instances Ford encourages the culprits to overact their confessions as if catharsis were a function of the most agonizing atonement, again suggesting a religious quest for absolutes rather than a humanist acceptance of ambiguities.

After *Stagecoach* and *Young Mr Lincoln*, Ford was entitled to a drop-off with *Drums Along the Mohawk*, his first film in colour and his only film to deal with the Revolutionary War period. The film is not without its stirring set pieces of ill-assorted settlers coalescing into a national army, and the James Fenimore Cooper horseless and foresty Indians are impressively cunning and menacing, but the film never recovers from Claudette Colbert's whining performance at the outset of her ordeal in the wilderness. Fonda's foot-race with two Indian pursuers, and Edna May Oliver's patterned *grande dame* heroics help make the movie entertaining enough, but the extensive

Young Mr Lincoln: courtroom theatrics

detail of the Walter Edmonds novel and the woman's point of view
embodied in top-billed Claudette Colbert and co-scenarist Sonya
Levien (with Lamarr Trotti) were probably more than Ford felt he
could handle conscientiously within one movie. *Drums Along the
Mohawk*, like *How Green Was My Valley* and *Seven Women*, was
conceived more in matriarchal than in patriarchal terms. But as we
shall see, Ford was more successful later in reconciling his patriarchal prejudices with uncongenial material than he is here in 1939 on
the eve of his greatest critical triumph, *The Grapes of Wrath*, the film
that was single-handedly to transform him from a storyteller of the
screen to America's cinematic poet laureate.

3: 1940–1947: The Poet Laureate

Who is the actual (or even predominant) author of a film? This question had perplexed film scholars long before *auteurism* added a new dimension to the debate. (*Vide* the voluminous brief filed in the expressionist camera case of Murnau *vs.* Mayer.) Even when we stipulate multiple authorship in a collaborative art-form, we find that the problem has not been solved. Certainly, *The Grapes of Wrath* could not have become a motion picture if Darryl F. Zanuck or some other producer had not willed it into being by purchasing the rights to John Steinbeck's novel. The next-in-command after Zanuck was associate producer–scenarist Nunnally Johnson, who adapted the novel into a screenplay for John Ford to direct. Ford, in turn, worked very closely with Gregg Toland on the camera set-ups, but there was a great deal of second-unit work as well, and the final editing was very much a studio operation. But even if we could imagine a single ego which encompassed all the creative and productive functions represented by the names Steinbeck, Zanuck, Johnson, Ford, Toland *et al.*, we would still be confronted with the autonomous assertions of the players on the screen, not only on the stellar level of Henry Fonda's Tom Joad nor on the archetypal level of Jane Darwell's Ma Joad, nor on the grizzled grandeur level of Charles Grapewin's Grampa Joad, nor on the messianic level of John Carradine's Casey, but down also to such cameo gems as Paul Guilfoyle's wry-mouthed born troublemaker and Grant Mitchell's benignly tut-tutting New Deal bureaucrat.

We would be confronted also with the vast area of affecting accident recorded by the camera for display on a canvas which extends in both space and time. Even the constituent viewer elements of the editorial 'we' would provide a bewildering diversity of viewpoints and associations, and the passage of time would actually alter the 'look', 'sound' and 'feel' of the film. When *The Grapes of Wrath* was screened for students at a Yale seminar I gave in 1970, the hostile reaction baffled me at first, but then I realized that what had seemed unusually courageous in 1940 seemed unduly contrived in 1970. And what had once seemed the last word in 'realism' now seemed strangely stylized. Besides, the New Dealish optimism which had initially inspired the project had evaporated over the years with the swings to the Right of McCarthyism, Eisenhowerism and Nixonism, and with the growing realization that the original Okies of *The Grapes of Wrath* were eventually to become the staunchest supporters of Ronald Reagan in California.

Rebecca Pulliam provides a thoughtfully radical critique of *The Grapes of Wrath* in *The Velvet Light Trap* (No. 2, August 1971), and concludes: 'As with the Protestant ethic and New Dealism, John Ford *à la* 1940 stays within certain safe limits of expression and does not assault the confines of its preconceptions any more than he penetrates the political organization. Certainly, a man cannot be blamed for the shortness of vision of his times. But the makers of this movie were unfortunately caught without a new vision – between decades and between myths.'

Of course, one can argue that few movies of any decade or any country can be said to be genuinely radical in opposition to the social substance upon which they feed. Eisenstein dutifully excluded Trotsky from the October Revolution in *October*, and one would search in vain for any signs of Hollywood pacifism between Pearl Harbour and Hiroshima. Even so, Ford's conservative evolution in the Fifties and Sixties has misled modern film historians into theorizing about a conservative conspiracy back in 1940 to subvert Steinbeck's scathing critique of American society by substituting New Dealish homilies. It all depends upon one's frame of reference. Compared with other Hollywood movies of 1940, *The Grapes of Wrath* does not seem conservative at all; compared with the writings of Che Guevara and Eldridge Cleaver, it seems more like a hymn to honky capitalism and rugged individualism.

Even so, it would be a mistake to view the alleged betrayal of a sacred literary source in purely ideological terms. Steinbeck's 'choric interludes', which Ms. Pulliam considers crucial to Steinbeck's cosmic conception of suffering humanity, would have loaded down the screen with much the same kind of rhetorical bombast which characterized D. W. Griffith's universal brotherhood superimpositions in *Birth of a Nation*, and his recurring refrain of Lillian Gish's (and Walt Whitman's) 'Cradle Endlessly Rocking' in *Intolerance*. Indeed, Steinbeck's 'choric interludes' seem today only to increase the novelist's biological distance from his protagonists, who, by absorption into the mass of abstract mankind, become a small detachment of lowly marchers in a veritable army of avenging ants on the picnic blankets of the bourgeoisie. A very pitying expression of liberal guilt, to be sure, but hardly the heady stuff of which revolutions are made. It is perhaps more than a coincidence that both Steinbeck and John Dos Passos, from whose 'newsreel' and 'camera eye' in *U.S.A.* Steinbeck had borrowed his choric interludes, turned conservative in their later years, thus reflecting the ultimate rupture between the New Deal-Old Left of one generation and the New Left of another.

Back in 1940, however, the problem of adapting Steinbeck's novel to the screen must have been one more of poetics than of politics. We are a long way from Theodore Dreiser's ideological commitment to Eisenstein over Sternberg for the film version of *An American Tragedy*. Still, even Eisenstein with all his clickety-clackety montage never demonstrated how a long novel could be faithfully adapted into a short movie. As it is, *The Grapes of Wrath* runs for 129 minutes, not too long by the one-shot standard of *Gone With the Wind*, but appreciably longer than the slightly under 91 minute average running time of Ford's twenty-six features in the Thirties. Also, the evolving rationale of Hollywood screenwriting had become progressively less talkie-oriented all through the Thirties. Ford, especially, had become a legend on the set for replacing preciously literary lines with eloquent silences. The trick was to find the visual equivalents for wordy plots. Don't tell 'em, show 'em. Indeed, most critics had been brainwashed by highbrow aestheticians into believing that talk was the mortal enemy of cinema as an art-form. Hence, the process of reducing and simplifying a novel for the screen enjoyed the highest aesthetic sanction.

Modernist film aestheticians like Jean-Luc Godard and Roland Barthes can debate the contrasting ideologies of words and images, but in the Forties there was very little critical precedent for examining the tensions between word and image, screenwriter and director, content and form, substance and style. There could be a disparity of effectiveness, but not a disparity of meaning. Thus critics could applaud John Ford's stylistic contribution to *The Grapes of Wrath* without suggesting in any way that he was undermining the thematic thrust of John Steinbeck's novel and Nunnally Johnson's screenplay. That there could be an ideological contradiction between the beautiful pictures of Ford and Toland and the angry words of Steinbeck and Johnson would have seemed as strange a notion in 1940 as any similar critique of the stylistic beauties of the neo-realistic films would have seemed a decade later. At the very least, Ford and Toland could be charged by a retroactively revolutionary tribunal with diminishing the urgency of this enterprise with their eye-catching compositions of light and shadow on windswept fields and weather-beaten faces. There is even a ceiling (of a diner) photographed a full year before *Citizen Kane*, and a novelistic flashback shortly before *Rebecca* and a year before *How Green Was My Valley*. Thus another film classic turns out to be more expressionist than its realist reputation would indicate. The term used to circumvent this stylistic contradiction is 'poetic realism'.

Only long after the event has it become possible to conclude that Ford's personal concerns were particularly inimical to Steinbeck's conception of his characters. Whereas Steinbeck depicted oppression by dehumanizing his characters into creatures of abject necessity, Ford evoked nostalgia by humanizing Steinbeck's economic insects into heroic champions of an agrarian order of family and community. But both Steinbeck and Ford share a kind of half-baked faith in the verities of outhouse existence, and a sentimental mistrust of machinery. Neither Steinbeck nor Ford would have fitted very comfortably in the Soviet scheme of things with its worship of industrialization. But the early Forties were years of Popular Front sentimentality once the embarrassment of the Nazi–Soviet pact had been forgotten and forgiven, and in this ecumenical era it did not seem too far-fetched to link the rural evangelism in *The Grapes of Wrath* with world revolution. After all, more seemed to be at stake than a crass studio's desire to make money from a downbeat project. The minds and hearts of the moviegoing masses were thought to be hanging in the balance. Why alienate these masses needlessly by reproducing Steinbeck's vision of existence as a dunghill of despair?

The Grapes of Wrath: 'heroic champions of an agrarian order'

The Grapes of Wrath: 'their coherence as a family'

In hindsight, we might note that only a Luis Buñuel at his most outrageous would be capable of rendering all the gruesome horror of Steinbeck's saga on the relatively squeamish screen. But what would Buñuel have evoked with lurid fidelity to Steinbeck, tacticians of the time might have asked, beyond the nervous laughter of the sophisticates and the revulsion of the general public? By contrast, the strategy tacitly agreed upon by Zanuck, Johnson and Ford enabled the audience to identify itself with the sufferings of the characters, partly by making these characters active rather than passive, partly by stressing their coherence as a family though not as a class, and partly by offering hope in the future through Jane Darwell's concluding we-the-people speech, in its own way almost as controversial as Charles Chaplin's world-peace speech in *The Great Dictator*. Still, it is worth remembering that Odetsian audiences in Manhattan balconies cheered wildly in the Forties when Ma Joad dispensed her populist manifesto: 'Rich fellas come up an' they die, an' their kids ain't no good, an' they die out. But we keep a-comin'. We're the people that live. Can't nobody wipe us out. Can't nobody lick us. We'll go on forever.'

Resounding rhetoric aside, *The Grapes of Wrath* is graced with subtler virtues than its dated 'message' would indicate. After being overrated in its time as a social testament, it is now underrated both as a Hollywood movie (not glossily mythic enough) and as a Ford memento (not purely personal enough). What *does* stand up to every test of time, however, is Henry Fonda's gritty incarnation of Tom Joad, a volatile mixture of the prairie sincerity of *Young Mr Lincoln* with the snarling paranoia of Fritz Lang's *You Only Live Once*. Once more, Fonda was passed over for top acting honours by both the Academy and the New York Film Critics. Possibly, his was too unsettling a performance for facile audience identification. Fonda–Joad's physical and spiritual stature is not that of the little man as victim, but of the tall man as troublemaker. His explosive anger has a short fuse, and we have only his word for it that he is tough without being mean. Indeed, it is mainly his awkwardness in motion that suggests his vulnerability, but there is a tendency in the devious blankness of his expression to make him seem more sullen than he has any right or motivation to be. Consequently, his putatively proletarian hero becomes morosely menacing in that shadowy crossroads where social justice intersects with personal vengeance. Fonda's Joad is no Job, and as much as his mouth spouts slogans of equality, his hands are always reaching for a club or a rock or a wrench as an equalizer against the social forces massed against him. His is ultimately the one-man revolution of the ex-con with whom society can never be reconciled. By contrast, Jane Darwell's Ma Joad is the pacifier and unifier and high priestess of liberal reform at the altar of the sacred family.

Even within the Joad family, however, the significantly generational conflict between Charley Grapewin's Grampa Joad and Jane Darwell's Ma Joad is generally misunderstood and misinterpreted as the affectionate squabbling of quaintly rural types. But what is

The Grapes of Wrath: Fonda as Tom Joad

actually happening is nothing less than the transformation of the
Joad family from a patriarchy rooted in the earth to a matriarchy
uprooted on the road. It is no accident, even in the casting, that
Charley Grapewin's Grampa dominates Zeffie Tilbury's Grandma
Joad as completely as Jane Darwell's Ma Joad dominates Russell
Simpson's Pa Joad. Once on the road, the men have a tendency to
wander and finally run away altogether either via drink or via
distance. The women of the family must then hold the fort and save
the children as poverty and unemployment destroy the authority of
the paterfamilias.

Ford's own feelings are so powerfully patriarchal that when
Grampa dies, something in the movie seems to die with him. Hence
the complaint of many critics that the first third of *The Grapes of
Wrath* is superior to the final two-thirds. Parker Tyler noted astutely
that even the surface of the screen seemed to change from lyrical
dustiness to an antiseptic enamel finish. Ford's concern with the
sacraments of the soil is expressed in the poetically sifting hands of

John Qualen's maddened Muley and Grampa himself, and it is in this primal property gesture that we sense the conservative commitment of Ford's feelings to the dirt shrivelled by the wind into dust, but still drenched in all its dryness with the blood, sweat and tears of generations. Later, in *They Were Expendable*, Ford even redeems Russell Simpson (who is so diminished in *The Grapes of Wrath*) by making him Dad, chief of the shipyard, and a haunting hold-out who sits on his porch with his rifle perched on his lap, and his dog poised by his side, waiting, waiting, waiting for the invading Japanese. As doggedly loyal-to-the-land Dad, Russell Simpson restores the patriarchy which disappeared in *The Grapes of Wrath* somewhere on the road between Oklahoma and California.

The Long Voyage Home marked Ford's penultimate collaboration with Dudley Nichols, and the film is suitably moody, shadowy and romantically fatalistic for the occasion. The narrative is very slight, as befits an adaptation of four Eugene O'Neill one-act plays: *Bound East for Cardiff* (1916), *In the Zone* (1917), *The Long Voyage Home* (1917), *The Moon of the Caribbees* (1918). Peter Bogdanovich reports that the Ford–Nichols adaptation was 'O'Neill's favourite among the films made of his work, and the only one he looked at periodically'. We are back in the familiar Ford–Nichols domain of *Men Without Women*, a particularly poetic realm for film critics who seemed unduly impressed by the mere absence of Hollywood boy-meets-girl conventions. As it happens, *The Long Voyage Home* has dated worse than *The Grapes of Wrath*. Its collective saga of men at sea seems arbitrarily austere most of the time, and yet unexpectedly maudlin at its big moments. Ian Hunter's 'Smitty', an upper-class outcast, is cut from the same sentimentally redemptive cloth as Kenneth McKenna's 'Burke' in *Men Without Women*, Reginald Denny's George Brown in *The Lost Patrol*, and John Carradine's Hatfield in *Stagecoach*. But never before has this stock character seemed so obtrusive in a Ford film.

Part of the problem may be that *The Long Voyage Home* represents a conscious extension of the foggy expressionism of the Thirties into the programmed heroics of World War II. Producer Walter Wanger, Ford and Nichols were all outspokenly anti-Hitler in this period, and thus *The Long Voyage Home* constituted a conscious tribute to Britain in its darkest hour against the Nazi

The Long Voyage Home: 'moody, shadowy and romantically fatalistic'

hordes, who here invade O'Neill's brooding seascapes with an air strike from out of nowhere. British critics C. A. Lejeune and Lindsay Anderson found Ford's flourish of the Union Jack on Smitty's coffin an unspeakably vulgar gesture, but Ford has always transformed flag-waving into a personal figure of style, be the flag the Union Jack, the Stars and Stripes (*The Battle of Midway, They Were Expendable*) or that of the Irish Republic (*The Plough and the Stars*).

The redeeming twitches of idiosyncratic low-life are provided by a strong cast of character actors headed by the ubiquitous bulldog conscience of the era, Thomas Mitchell, and featuring John Wayne in one of the strangest parts of his career as the oafish Scandinavian innocent Ole Olsen, who is almost shanghaied by that oddest of all tavern wenches, Mildred Natwick's Freda. Actually, the most haunting passage of the film is the idyllic opening with its caressingly illuminated native women canoeing and carousing with the susceptible men of the S.S. *Glencairn*. By contrast, the end of the voyage on the fog-shrouded London docks marks also the end of all the men's illusions of life on shore. In this respect, Ford and O'Neill are kindred spirits in that they share a tragic vision of life even though that vision is not as keenly articulated as that of the greatest tragedians of the past. It is a uniquely American–Irish-Catholic vision in which guilt, repression and submission play a large part.

Tobacco Road struck a slightly sour note in the triumphant blast of trumpets for Ford through 1940 and 1941. The general impression at the time was that this project was not worthy of a director of Ford's stature. Whereas *The Grapes of Wrath* extolled the nobility of the deserving poor, *Tobacco Road* exploited the nuttiness of the undeserving poor. In this Fordian context, Charley Grapewin's white-trash Jeeter Lester was an especially embarrassing parody of his Grampa in *The Grapes of Wrath*. Erskine Caldwell's sub-Zolaesque novel of demented rural refuse in Georgia was not without a certain degree of social significance and erotic élan for its time, but on its way to the screen it stopped off in 1933 for a very profitable run on the Broadway stage in a hoked-up theatrical adaptation by Jack Kirkland.

Unfortunately, the Hollywood Production Code tolerated neither Caldwell's flair for bawdiness nor Kirkland's for boisterous bathroom humour, with the result that Ford and Nunnally Johnson had to perform prodigious feats of ellipsis to get the material on the screen at all. Gene Tierney's stylized barnyard crawl as the lustful Ellie May Lester typified the film's balletic sublimation of the novel's blatant sexuality. Moreover, William Tracy's excruciatingly strident Dude Lester suggested that Ford had devised loudness as a comic substitute for lewdness. Tracy's more controlled performances in Ernst Lubitsch's *Shop Around the Corner* and Busby Berkeley's *Strike Up the Band* would seem to serve as a rebuke to Ford's broadness in *Tobacco Road*. On the other hand, Ford's extraordinarily sympathetic treatment of the elder Lesters (Grapewin, Elizabeth Patterson as Ada his mate, and Zeffie Tilbury as the rebelliously disappearing Grandma Lester) transcends barnyard farce with bucolic fantasy. The parts may not cohere, but the sombre mood is triumphantly Fordian. Shortly after World War II, the Tito regime in Yugoslavia decided to release *The Grapes of Wrath* and *Tobacco Road* throughout the country in order to demonstrate that the United States was no longer a land of great opportunity. Ironically,

Fordian families: (*above*) *The Grapes of Wrath*; (*below*) *Tobacco Road*

Yugoslav audiences were so enthralled by all the motor vehicles on the screen that this supposedly Marxist double feature was quickly withdrawn from distribution.

How Green Was My Valley has suffered the dubious distinction of being remembered as the film that beat out *Citizen Kane* for an Academy Award. The Oscars have seldom served as a reliable index of cinematic quality, and least of all when an eccentric talent like Orson Welles' was concerned. None the less it can be argued that, apart from *Sunrise* in 1927–8, *How Green Was My Valley* was the most meritorious movie ever to win an Academy Award. Unfortunately, the film so closely expressed the emotional climate of its time that it seems to have dated badly. Even a Ford admirer like Lindsay Anderson expressed grave reservations only a decade later: 'The film ... set Ford the impossible task of recreating on the Fox lot, with a mingled cast of English, American and Irish players, a mining village in early twentieth-century Wales. *How Green Was My Valley* was a "prestige" commercial picture (which Ford took over from William Wyler in the early stages of preparation), produced in the most lavish style and with decorative but almost entirely superficial mastery. It is typical that this film won more "Oscars" (a total of six, including one for its direction) than any other in Ford's career.'

Curiously, Philip Dunne's screenplay (from Richard Llewellyn's novel) conspicuously failed to win an Oscar for 1941, that questionable honour going to Herman J. Mankiewicz and Orson Welles for the now very controversial screenplay for *Kane*. And yet of all Ford's films, *How Green Was My Valley* was the one most strongly shaped by a novelistic screenplay. Some time in the Forties it became suddenly fashionable to tell a story on the screen with the help of a very fanciful narrator and a very intricate flashback structure. *Rebecca, The Great McGinty, Kitty Foyle, Penny Serenade, A Woman's Face, I Wake Up Screaming, Yankee Doodle Dandy, The Magnificent Ambersons, Heaven Can Wait, The Hard Way, So Proudly We Hail, Laura, Double Indemnity, It's a Wonderful Life, The Killers, The Moon and Sixpence, The Great Moment, The Lost Weekend, et al.* made the screen more sonorous all through the Forties than it had been at any time in the Thirties. There were many factors involved in this stylistic trend. Early in 1940 Preston Sturges launched a writer-to-director movement, the scope of which was unparalleled in Hollywood's history. After Sturges led the way, John Huston, Billy Wilder, Clifford Odets, Robert Rossen, Samuel Fuller, Frank Tashlin, Blake Edwards and such Ford collaborators as Dudley Nichols, Nunnally Johnson and Philip Dunne eventually found their way from the writer's cubicle to the director's chair. And as the Screenwriter's Guild achieved more authority and autonomy within the film industry, the word became the expressive equal of the image.

Of course, flashbacks date back to the very early Griffith and Ince features before 1920. With the coming of sound in the late Twenties, however, film-makers developed a very intense resistance to any form of verbal narration. Music could be played only in the visual presence of realistic 'sources', and printed subtitles or intertitles were the preferred means of imparting time-place-theme information as opposed to a voice-over, however mellifluous. Why then did Hollywood suddenly overcome its fear of losing its supposed chastity as a 'visual art form'? The highbrow explanation may dwell on the impact of the novel on films in this period, but a more likely influence on the aural receptivity of both studios and audiences was the very popular forms of radio storytelling, notably Cecil B. DeMille's Lux Radio Theatre, which adapted popular movies into flashback structures for Mr DeMille's fatherly narration; the Nigel Bruce–Basil Rathbone enactments of the Sherlock Holmes stories with Bruce's evenly cadenced prose passages introducing and concluding each episode; the Orson Welles broadcasts, particularly his Martian coup; and innumerable other programmes in which the spoken word cast a spell on listeners.

Through most of his career Ford had employed narration even more sparingly than dialogue. In this context, *How Green Was My Valley* seems particularly alien to Ford's patented brand of laconic lyricism. Not only was he dealing with a culture completely foreign to him; he was evoking a past he had never felt first-hand. Still, there have probably been more tears shed over *How Green Was My Valley* than over any other Ford film. We cannot say that Ford himself earned all these tears with the fruits of his own sensibility. The pathos of pastness embodied in the Dunne–Llewellyn narrative must take much of the credit. What Ford contributed above everything else was the tenacity of family feelings, and the awesome irrevocability of archetypal experiences. It is difficult to see how Wyler could

How Green Was My Valley: 'the pathos of pastness' (Roddy MacDowall, Donald Crisp)

have achieved a comparable explosion of emotion even with identical material. When one recalls the remarkable coolness of such surefire tear-jerkers as *Wuthering Heights* and *Mrs Miniver*, one realizes that Wyler's polish and perfectionism were made of sterner stuff than Ford's intuitive involvement. I have never known anyone who could remain dry-eyed through Roddy McDowall's desperate search through the flooded mineshaft for his trapped father (Donald Crisp). Here again was the misty realm of family epic to which Ford so often gravitated.

We must remember, however, that the archetypal characters and situations would not have seemed so moving to audiences and critics in 1941 were it not for an emotional correlation between memories of a Welsh mining family earlier in the century and the more immediate impressions of the Great Depression from which America was only now emerging in order to prepare for the Great War. In this context, *How Green Was My Valley* served almost as a sequel to *The Grapes of Wrath*. There were the same conflicts between capital and labour, the same spectacles of social injustice, the same strains on the fabric of the family and the same intimations of indomitability among the poeticized poor. There were differences as well. Thus whereas *The Grapes of Wrath* was filmed in the present imperative, *How Green Was My Valley* was filmed in the past indefinite. By the end of 1941 Americans could almost look back on the Depression as a collective saga now safely concluded. Within one year the cry for

105

How Green Was My Valley: the mine disaster

reform in *The Grapes of Wrath* could give way to the chant of remembrance in *How Green Was My Valley*. The colourful Welsh with their melodious chorales transcended their studio sets (the same sloping mining village used a year later for *The Moon Is Down*) to become the glorious poor of all nations.

It was perhaps the last time that an American film could identify its own emotional concerns so intimately with those of the common run of humanity. Neo-realism was still only a gleam in the eye of a handful of Italian film-makers, and the Russian cinema had long since abandoned egalitarianism for statism, peasant for Tsar, the end of St Petersburg for the defence of Stalingrad. The French cinema under the German Occupation was entering its Cocteau–Carné– Prévert period of stylish sleepwalking that would culminate in *Les Enfants du Paradis*. England was only just hitting its stride with its wartime documentaries. Thus, Hollywood stood alone for a brief moment in history as the hope of the world, the champion of the common man, and the defender of democratic values. Later in the Forties

Hollywood would be made to seem frivolous and irresponsible, but at the time of the release of *How Green Was My Valley* there was no industry inferiority complex to speak of. Nor was the dead hand of the past a demoralizing factor. Movies seemed truly better than ever, and even the New York film critics had been unusually sanguine about the future of the American cinema ever since *The Grapes of Wrath* had burst on the screen in early 1940. John Ford was named best director by both the Academy and the Film Critics for both 1940 and 1941, over such formidable competition as Chaplin, Welles, Wyler, Hitchcock, Lubitsch, Sturges, Hawkes, Cukor, Lang, Huston, Stevens, Capra *et al.* The awards to Ford were sincerely granted. People at the time genuinely believed that *How Green Was My Valley* was a better movie than *Citizen Kane*. It was warmer, more disciplined, less flamboyant and less self-indulgent, in short, a repository of the classical virtues in contrast to the romantic vices of *Kane*.

In the Fifties André Bazin and Roger Leenhardt would conclude that Welles and Wyler had launched the modern cinema's adventure in ambiguity with the single-take deep focus probes of *Citizen Kane* and *The Little Foxes*. 'Vive, Wyler! A bas, Ford!' was the belated battle cry of the Bazin–Leenhardt critical cabal on *Revue du Cinéma* and *Cahiers du Cinéma*, belated because the French had not seen the American Forties films until after the German Occupation in 1945. Yet, Gregg Toland, the cinematographer on both *Kane* for Welles and *Foxes* for Wyler, lamented publicly in 1941 that he had not been assigned to Ford for *How Green Was My Valley*. And when we look today at *How Green Was My Valley* with a stylistically unjaundiced eye, we can appreciate some stunning deployments of family members in deep focus and even deeper rapport. Two especially exquisite manifestations of family feeling involve Donald Crisp's head-lowering reaction in the foreground to the wistful memory-beyond-death sentiments uttered in the background by the bravely bereaved womenfolk (Anna Lee, Sara Allgood).

It was an oddity even in its time that the audience never sees the grown-up narrator on the screen. Peter Bogdanovich credits Rhys Williams with the narration. If Williams does indeed read the narration, I remain perpetually surprised. My image of the narrator was always that of a young, good-looking, cultivated man, rather than the middle-aged character type in the movie who plays the blind boxer, Dai Bando. We somehow never feel that we are looking across as vast a continent of time as separates the present from the past in the Losey–Pinter–Hartley *The Go-Between*. It is at least partly a matter of the difference in perspective between the communal past celebrated in the Ford–Dunne–Llewellyn *Valley* and the personal past mourned in *The Go-Between*. It may be the difference also between lost roots and lost innocence.

Viewed purely as a mineshaft movie, *How Green Was My Valley* did not dig very deeply for the kind of ideological ironies one finds in G. W. Pabst's *Kamaradschaft* (Franco-German fraternity) and Carol Reed's *The Stars Look Down* (Capital versus Labour). There is an air of religious resignation in Ford's treatment of the climactic disaster sequence as Sara Allgood's now widowed matriarch looks upwards at the heavens to acknowledge the ascension of her husband's soul from the muddy depths of the mine below her feet. By contrast, the trapped miners in *Kamaradschaft* and *The Stars Look Down* claw at the entombing walls to gain the light of life on this earth. There is no hereafter for Marxist miners; there is only the here and the now. But for Ford there is an unbroken chain of feelings between the living and the dead. Hence, the epilogue of *How Green Was My Valley* reunites a family fragmented by deaths and departures. Ford's ghosts are not the memory images imparted to Victor Sjöström's old professor in Ingmar Bergman's *Wild Strawberries*, but mystical incarnations of an unchanging world beyond the valley of death.

Ford is less successful in expressing visually and emotionally the film's matriarchal maxim: 'If our father was the head of the house, our mother was its heart.' Here it is Donald Crisp's father who prevails poetically over Sara Allgood's mother. Indeed, the emotional authority of the mother is fatally undermined when her youngest son Huw (the film's point-of-view narrator) chooses to abandon her in order to live with and support his widowed sister-in-law (Anna Lee), for whom he feels a childhood longing of an extraordinary delicacy. Even so, the boy's attachments to his beloved sister-in-law, his sainted mother and his beautiful sister (Maureen O'Hara) are very weak and wordy in comparison with the eloquent silences he shares with his father and his brothers.

Curiously, the film's central plot, which concerns the ill-starred love between Walter Pidgeon's penniless, well-spoken minister, Mr Gruffydd, and Maureen O'Hara's impetuous miner's daughter,

Angharad Morgan, has always seemed peripheral to the saga of the Morgan family. The film marked Pidgeon's interesting middle period between his early emergence as an inoffensive musical comedy lead and his later embalming with Greer Garson in Metro's Great Couple series. And Maureen O'Hara, a flaming red-haired Irish beauty, had hitherto been typed in roles of erotic masochism for such interestingly morbid romances as Alfred Hitchcock's *Jamaica Inn*, William Dieterle's *The Hunchback of Notre Dame* and Dorothy Arzner's *Dance, Girl, Dance*. But it was only in the films of John Ford that Maureen O'Hara acquired any sort of dramatic dimension. Here, unfortunately, the Pidgeon–O'Hara love scenes (with Roddy McDowall's Huw as the go-between) become overly rhetorical because Ford is unable in this context and in this period to project the sexual hunger of the Maureen O'Hara–John Wayne Fifties relationships in *The Quiet Man* and *Wings of Eagles*. In 1941, sexual hunger was hardly a fitting subject for America's cinematic poet laureate, and her leading exemplar of social consciousness.

After *How Green Was My Valley* Ford went on active duty in the Navy as Chief of the Field Photographic Branch, a unit of the Office of Strategic Services (later glorified on the screen as the O.S.S.) with offices in Paris and London. Among the Hollywood hands Ford recruited for his documentary team were Gregg Toland, Garson Kanin, Budd Schulberg, Joseph Walker, Daniel Fuchs, Claude Dauphin, Robert Parrish, Jack Pennick and Ray Kellog. Ford was away from commercial film production for more than three years, but this abstinence was considered appropriate for an artist in his quasi-official position. He even picked up an extra Oscar for *The Battle of Midway*, America's first war documentary, and also a Purple Heart for wounds incurred in the engagement. This was shooting in both senses of the word.

Of course, many other Hollywood directors went to war, among them Stevens, Wyler, Huston and Capra. It seemed the thing to do at the time. World War II was a war with something for everybody: racism (against the treacherous Nipponese abroad and the helpless Nisei at home) for the American Right, anti-Fascism (in the European Theatre) for the American Left, and good old-fashioned patriotism for the American Centre. When Ford and Toland recorded the raising of the American flag on Midway in the midst of the Japanese attack, every American could cheer without any ideological reservations. The flag was not yet the divisive emblem it was to become during the Vietnam War. But Ford's allegiances never wavered. He is the only American film director who lent his artistic services to the Government through World War II, the Korean War and the Vietnam War. The two latter wars were as divisive as World War II was unifying. And even by the end of World War II, Ford's communal, patriotic attitude towards war was beginning to fall out of favour with the cultural establishment. Thus when Ford returned to Hollywood to film *They Were Expendable* in 1945, he was already out of synch with the prevailing *Zeitgeist*.

By any standard it was not a triumphal return. Not only was the war over by the time (late December, 1945) *They Were Expendable* went into release; the film dealt with the very early misadventures of the war almost four years before. What could have seemed more perverse than Ford's celebration of gallant defeat in the aftermath of glorious victory? It was as if the director had become nostalgic for certain values he felt slipping away irretrievably in the noisily opportunist postwar world. Indeed, there was something anachronistic back in 1945 in Ford's invocations of unquestioning self-sacrifice, a dogged devotion to duty, an ingrained sense of responsibility, and a transcendental faith in a nation's worthiness to accept the fearsome sacrifices of its expendable individuals.

In his review of the film in *The Nation* (5 January, 1946) James Agee perceived a directorial sensibility at work on slightly dubious material:

For what seems at least half of the dogged, devoted length of *They Were Expendable* all you have to watch is men getting on or off PT boats, and other men watching them do so. But this is made so beautiful and so real that I could not feel one foot of the film was being wasted. The rest of the time the picture is showing nothing much newer, with no particular depth of feeling, much less idea; but, again, the whole thing is so beautifully directed and photographed, in such an abundance of vigorous open air and good raw sunlight, that I thoroughly enjoyed and admired it. Visually, and in detail, and in nearly everything he does with people, I think it is John Ford's finest movie. Another man who evidently learned a tremendous amount through the war is Robert Montgomery, whose sober, light, sure performance is, so far as I can remember, the one perfection to turn up in movies during the year.

They Were Expendable

Yet, only two weeks later (in *The Nation* of 19 January, 1946), Agee decided that *They Were Expendable*, though one of the better films of the year, was 'visually beautiful, otherwise not very interesting'. For top honours in 1945 Agee preferred 'Major' John Huston's *San Pietro* and William Wellman's *Story of G.I. Joe*, both very morbid contemplations of the victorious Italian campaign in contrast to Ford's very heroic celebration of the ill-fated Philippine campaign. The handwriting was on the screen: Ford's days as a culture hero were numbered.

It is not that Ford was about to be supplanted by any other single director. Through the late Forties, the Fifties and the Sixties there was really no successor to Ford as cinematic poet laureate. Fred Zinnemann inherited some of Ford's reputation for realism and social virtue, but only intermittently. Elia Kazan's career flared up briefly in the Fifties, and then subsided. For the most part, the post of Hollywood poet laureate remained vacant. Hollywood itself lost its pre-war lustre, and at the end of 1946 the industry was shocked to discover that Bosley Crowther, the very influential critic of the *New York Times*, had listed five foreign films on his ten-best list. Ford's brand of realism now paled before the earthy, fuzzy, but none the less canny 'crudities' of the neo-realists, particularly Roberto Rossellini (*Open City, Paisà*) and Vittorio De Sica (*Shoeshine, Bicycle Thieves*). Ironically, Luchino Visconti, the one neo-realist director with whom Ford shared a certain stylistic elegance, never made it to

They Were Expendable: 'an image of man amid the rubble' (John Wayne, Ward Bond, Robert Montgomery)

American screens until the mid-Fifties, when the term neo-realism had degenerated into a derisive tagline for archaic mannerisms.

Of course, American audiences had been completely saturated with war propaganda by the time *They Were Expendable* was released. Errol Flynn alone had won World War II many times over as romance, sometimes very graceful but more often merely glossy, prevailed over grim, grubby realism. The bloodiest of the documentary war films were not released to audiences until after the war. *The Battle of San Pietro*, for example, has been seen by very few people even to this day, and John Huston's psychiatric study of shell-shock cases, *Let There Be Light*, by even fewer. Once the war was over, the war film tended to slide in social significance from a cause to a genre, from a statement of principles to a set of platitudes.

The Forties' critics had been obsessed by the war itself and its social convulsions to the point that a movie could never again be merely a movie but must instead aspire to the status of a social force. Agee was not alone in ascribing maturity to those Hollywood directors who had been privileged to participate in the war. It was a common refrain of the postwar era. Hollywood, like America, had supposedly joined the world at large, and the insular innocence and provincialism of the pre-war period was no longer an appropriate attitude. As movies of the Thirties and early Forties were glibly consigned to the attic of an American childhood, the imperatives of history decreed that Hollywood had to lead America into adulthood. Agee and Crowther, each in his own inimitable rhetoric, focused attention on the matter of film at the expense of the manner. As a result, a crisis of confidence spread through Hollywood as movies were viewed increasingly as feeble imitations of life rather than as self-contained fantasies of restructured reality. Agee was no stranger to directorial style as Crowther was, but his moralizing, like Crowther's, encouraged lesser critics to practise blind sermonizing in place of visual analysis.

If *They Were Expendable* has stood the test of time as one of Ford's most evocative works, it is less as history than as mythology. Indeed, the entire film can now be viewed as an elegy to doomed individuals in a common cause. Ford had come out of the war with an image of man amid the rubble, humanity amid the holocaust. We need not know if the cause be just or not. The fire and smoke, the death and destruction, the blood and tears, take us from Troy to Bataan and back in the never-ending epic of our race. And Ford's camera again stands back at an epic distance, for which he pays a price in the imprecision of his psychological delineation. Even his co-protagonists, Lt. John Brickley (Robert Montgomery) and Lt. Rusty Ryan (John Wayne), are conceived dramaturgically in conventional *What Price Glory* terms of bickering camaraderie. Fortunately Montgomery, with his refined edginess, and Wayne, with his raw energy, are never given time to develop trivial differences of outlook. Instead they are engulfed almost immediately (Pearl Harbour and all that) by events beyond their control, and their histrionically diverse temperaments are harmonized in tune with Ford's dominant thematic of defeat and self-abnegation.

Montgomery, much the smoother actor of the two, settles into a paternally stabilizing relationship with Wayne's slightly unruly child warrior; Montgomery a wary Odysseus, as it were, to Wayne's excitable Achilles. It follows with mythic logic that the Wayne character is the more susceptible of the two to injury. It follows also

113

that it would be the Montgomery character who would seem to be burdened with some prior obligations, perhaps by even a Penelope of sorts, whereas the Wayne character would be footloose and fancy free enough to begin a love affair (with Donna Reed's Lt. Sandy Davis) at the very edge of eternity, a liaison severed with awesome abruptness by a broken telephone connection. None the less, the shadowy images of Wayne and Reed as they ritualistically seek each other out are among the most intensely romantic images of love and death in the American cinema. Still, it seemed a little late in the day for a supposedly serious American director to be serenading the All-American Girl in Sternbergian patterns of light and shadow, courtesy of Joseph H. August's classical lenses.

By contrast, the earthier visions of Huston's *San Pietro* and Wellman's *The Story of G.I. Joe* did not envisage women explicitly, but left them latent in the longing, hungering faces of men at war. Huston and Wellman have always had a tendency in their manlier projects to treat women not in terms of Ford's chivalric idealism, but as necessary evils in relieving male frustration; *vide* the strikingly similar bits of business with a suggestive bar-room painting in Wellman's *The Oxbow Incident* and *Yellow Sky*, and the ostentatiously sluttish females at the fringes of just about every Huston movie. But only in wartime does male lust become ennobled as a significant symptom of the human condition. It is not that *San Pietro* and *The Story of G.I. Joe* were concerned primarily with this aspect of the war, but that they were taken more seriously than *They Were Expendable* largely because they eschewed the conventions of boy–girl romance. *San Pietro* seemed particularly impressive for not penetrating the awesome anonymity of the young American infantry-men marching up the mountain to certain death. As always, however, Huston tended to evade moral responsibility for the damning footage of this most botched-up of American campaigns. Indeed, General Mark Clark, the ill-famed American architect of the systematic annihilation of the American foot soldier, is actually introduced in the film as its narrator and raisonneur. Huston tried to have it both ways: War is Hell for the humanists; War is Noble for the patriots. Actually, Huston's sour, cynical, defeatist attitude towards human endeavour in *San Pietro* fell somewhere between the nihilism of his images and the nobility of their implications, somewhere between the mocking laughter of *The Treasure of the Sierra Madre* and the cold sweat of panic in *The Red Badge of Courage.* Agee, of course, was especially taken with Huston's awe-struck attitude towards the heartbreakingly real faces passing for an instant in his viewfinder before their rendezvous with death. Agee himself was later to fall under the spell of the morbid Huston mystique, with fatal consequences.

In the realm of fictional (as opposed to documentary) war films, *The Story of G.I. Joe* was regarded by most critics as decisively superior to *They Were Expendable.* For one thing, it was easier to isolate in one's memory the emotional high points in *The Story of G.I. Joe* than to reintegrate as an expressive whole the stylistic and spiritual fluidity of *They Were Expendable.*

Actually, *The Story of G.I. Joe* was more typical of Hollywood war films than *They Were Expendable* in that the Wellman version of the war focused more on individuals whereas the Ford version focused more on the group. Whereas *The Story of G.I. Joe* was constructed very loosely of ill-connected character vignettes, *They Were Expendable* flowed gracefully on an epic stream of collective destiny which allowed little leeway for individual psyches. The ethos of the team is expressed in *Expendable* by Montgomery's superior officer in the baseball parlance of being called upon to lay down a sacrifice bunt rather than to hit a home-run. By contrast, the G.I. Joes disdain the lofty rhetoric of duty and victory for the day-to-day exigencies of survival. It is interesting that both Ford and Hawks (*Air Force*) dealt with professional soldiers whereas Wellman and Milestone (*A Walk in the Sun*) dealt with citizen soldiers, indeed the thematic distinction between the nostalgic celebration in James Jones' *From Here to Eternity* and the cross-sectional dissection in Norman Mailer's *The Naked and the Dead.* It was the difference between believing that the war had conserved the old values, and affirming that the war had created new ones. It was the difference between going back and going forward. Ford was to go back.

Nothing is more symptomatic of Ford's falling out of step with the cultural establishment than his magnification of the MacArthur legend in *They Were Expendable.* As the General and his family are evacuated from Corregidor on the PT boats, Ford begins with a newsreel-like objective long shot, and then holds the General's figure in the frame until he ends up looming in close-up on the foredeck, sunglasses, corn-cob pipe and all. A young sailor asks the General for an autograph, and the film cuts to a comically exasperated Ward Bond, hurling his arms and his eyes to the heavens, the martial music blaring all the while. This gag sequencing of shots tends to conceal an apotheosis of the General. The timing of the sequence is really too quick for a lingering laugh, and the young sailor's indiscretion is designed quite obviously to lend a human dimension to a solemnly superhuman occasion. Even before the war was over, however, Douglas MacArthur had acquired a controversial reputation for his glory-seeking personality. His personal courage was questioned with the epithet of 'Dugout Doug', and he later became identified with the most reactionary elements of the Republican Party. Ford's artistic decision to treat MacArthur as if he were Lincoln was therefore politically premature. It was the superficially egalitarian Eisenhower who became the nation's unifying symbol as he went on to dismantle the New Deal in order to return America to the National Association of Manufacturers. By contrast, the majestic MacArthur, for all his strategic acumen, dwindled finally to a failed De Gaulle. Still, Ford could not help admiring the General's patrician style of pride and resistance in the face of a humiliating defeat. But the war was over, and it had become somewhat tasteless to continue glorifying a General who was grandiose to begin with.

Another revealing aspect of *They Were Expendable* is Ford's paternalist treatment of young men. The autograph incident is only the most spectacular example of his association of youth with rash immaturity rather than with idealistic rebellion. In the world of John Ford the young must learn from their elders, and the process is painfully and ridiculously slow. But by the same token, it is the sacred responsibility of the elders to look after the young and to teach them to survive. It is not likely that Ford could ever have accommodated such modishly alienated actors of the Fifties as Montgomery Clift, Marlon Brando and James Dean. It would be all he could do to keep Jeffrey Hunter under control as the wildest of all his semi-juveniles.

Ford's next project after *They Were Expendable* was *My Darling Clementine*, only his second Western in twenty years; and it is significant that Ford's decline in critical esteem tended to coincide with his return to the Old West on a regular basis. In this respect, *My Darling Clementine* is the work more of a poet laureate than of a poet, a Western for viewers with little interest in the genre. It is a Western also in which the realistic touches outweigh the romantic flourishes, and in which the plot is merely a pretext to document the period. Consequently, the final confrontation of the Earps and Doc Holliday on one side, and the Clantons on the other, seems almost anticlimactic. Ford's leisurely narrative style is at odds with the malignant Manicheism of the revenge plot. Indeed, Walter Brennan's Old Man Clanton was the most evil character in the Ford *oeuvre* until Charles Kemper's Uncle Shiloh Clegg in *Wagonmaster* four years later. Both Old Man Clanton and Uncle Shiloh Clegg live just long enough to see all their grown-up sons gunned down by the avengers of law and order and morality. The respective avengers (Henry Fonda's Wyatt Earp and Ben Johnson's Travis Blue) try to refrain from using firearms, but they are finally roused to action by a senseless murder. In *My Darling Clementine*, it is the revenge murder of an Earp in return for the death of a Clanton which sets up the climactic Gunfight at the O.K. Corral, a historical occurrence previously celebrated on a B-picture budget and against a cheesecloth background in Allan Dwan's 1939 *Frontier Marshal*. By contrast, Ford's staging of the gunfight is three-dimensional, with wind and dust for realistic atmosphere. And it is the Ford movie which caused Wyatt Earp and Doc Holliday to recur so frequently in Westerns of the Fifties and Sixties.

What are most memorable, however, are not the confrontations and the gunfights. In fact, Ford virtually throws away a showdown between Earp and Holliday by shooting it (literally and figuratively) in long shot. Ford's Westerns never depended excessively on the machismo match-ups of quick draws, but rather on the normally neglected intervals between the gun-shots when men received haircuts, courted their sweethearts, and even partook of fragments of frontier culture. Alan Mowbray's Granville Thorndyke, a soused Shakespearian actor, pops up so prominently in *Clementine* that we are reminded once more of a certain degree of self-consciousness in Ford's depiction of his action characters. Ford's people very often seem aware that they are striking a pose for posterity, or having their existence on earth preserved for all time on a daguerreotype. But even as they preen themselves in all their pompous pastness, they scratch around for the nagging necessities of survival. Their clothes itch and their stomachs growl, and time hangs heavy on their hands.

117

'Fragments of a frontier culture': Alan Mowbray and (*below*) Henry Fonda and Cathy Downs in *My Darling Clementine*

Hence, Ford's penchant for directing away from the obligatory action climaxes towards the optional Waiting-for-God-knows-what interludes.

It follows that what Ford makes us remember most vividly about Henry Fonda's Wyatt Earp in *Clementine* is not Earp's skill with a gun, but his lack of skill on a dance floor. And not merely Earp's, but Fonda's as well. Ford had been taken with Fonda's jolting awkwardness in the square dance in *The Grapes of Wrath*, and he resolved then and there to exploit the humanizing potential of Fonda's lurch-steps on every possible future occasion. But then of all the red-blooded Hollywood action directors, Ford was always the most enamoured of the dance as the most sacred of all social rituals. The sustained camera movement which follows Henry Fonda's Wyatt Earp round a corner to court his darling Clementine (Cathy Downs) and take her to a dance on the floor of an unfinished church tends to consecrate what is clearly the film's ceremonial high point.

What is odd about this visual convergence of the constricting forces of Civilization, Christianity and Monogamous Virtue is how little regret Ford shows for the doomed anarchic spirit of the Wild West, epitomized in the Clantons and in Linda Darnell's tediously victimized and despised dance hall girl. Ultimately, *My Darling Clementine* suffers grievously from an imbalance between the nice girl of Cathy Downs and the not-so-nice girl of Linda Darnell. For one thing, the iconographic content of the two actresses is out of all proportion to the dramatic content of their roles. The studio seems to have imposed Linda Darnell on Ford to the point of clogging his continuity with mystifying close-ups of Fox's rising star. Fortunately for Miss Darnell's career, she was only a couple of years away from more appreciative directors like Preston Sturges (*Unfaithfully Yours*) and Joseph L. Mankiewicz (*A Letter to Three Wives*). Otherwise, Ford's unsympathetic treatment of her in *My Darling Clementine* is comparable to his grudging toleration of Barbara Stanwyck in *The Plough and the Stars*. Similarly, Ford seemed far less creative in embellishing the romantic role of Victor Mature's Doc Holliday than he was in inventing memorable bits of business for Henry Fonda's Wyatt Earp. All in all, *My Darling Clementine* seems divided against itself as Ford's personal concerns struggle against Fox's more conventional concepts. Ford, poet laureate and all, had not yet completely broken the studio mould, and in the year when American

119

audiences and critics were mesmerized by *The Best Years of our Lives, Henry V* and *Open City*, John Ford seemed at best to be very pleasantly marking time with a quaintly old-fashioned genre.

Of *The Fugitive* (1947) Ford had this to say to Peter Bogdanovich: 'It came out the way I wanted it to – that's why it's one of my favourite pictures – to me, it was perfect. It wasn't popular. The critics got at it, and evidently it had no appeal to the public, but I was very proud of my work.' Among the critics who 'got at it' was Lindsay Anderson: 'Taking full advantage of his hard-won freedom from Front Office control, Ford shot it with (apparently) uncritical absolute self-indulgence, departing considerably from the script where the fancy took him. He turned out a long, ponderous film, whose slowness of pace was unsupported by any true dynamism of conception. Superbly photographed in a style of unrestrained opulence, its atmosphere was suffocatingly "arty"; and the actors were either poor or (in Fonda's case) plainly uncomfortable in their roles.'

James Agee (in the *Nation*) placed *The Fugitive* on his 1947 ten-best list, with Jean Vigo's *Zéro de Conduite*, Charles Chaplin's *Monsieur Verdoux*, Vittorio De Sica's *Shoeshine*, Luigi Zampa's *To Live in Peace*, and André Malraux's *Man's Hope* above it, and Elia Kazan's *Boomerang!*, David Lean's *Great Expectations*, Carol Reed's *Odd Man Out*, Sergei Eisenstein's *Ivan the Terrible*, Renè Clair's *Le Silence est d'or*, Jean Cocteau's *Beauty and the Beast*, and Edward Dmytryk's *Crossfire* below. None the less, Agee was remarkably ambivalent about Ford's achievement:

John Ford's *The Fugitive* is a solidly pro-Catholic picture about a priest, a creeping Jesus. My feelings about the Catholic Church are, to put it mildly, more mixed than Mr Ford's; I doubt that Jesus ever crept, and I am sickened when I watch others creep in His name; I dislike allegory and symbolism which are imposed on and denature reality as deeply as I love both when they bloom from and exalt reality; and romantic photography is the kind I care for least. Over all, I think *The Fugitive* is a bad work of art, tacky, unreal, and pretentious. Yet I think almost as highly of it as of the films mentioned above, because I have seldom seen in a moving picture such grandeur and sobriety of ambition, such continuous intensity of treatment or such frequent achievement of what was obviously worked for, however distasteful or misguided I think it.

The Fugitive: 'more painterly than poetic'

121

As it happened, *The Fugitive* marked the last occasion on which the great majority of American critics made the slightest effort to confront Ford as a contemporary artist. After *The Fugitive*, Ford was widely regarded as a voice from the past, as an eccentric antique dealer with a good eye for vintage Americana. And Ford seemed to respond to this benign neglect by becoming surlier and more self-indulgent. *The Fugitive* seemed to have been designed to recapture the mystical, expressionist aura of *The Informer*. Unfortunately, Ford's monumental treatment of the material tended to be pious rather than religious. Whereas Graham Greene's saintly sinner (in the novel *The Power and the Glory*) was cursed with faith despite all his cowardice and lechery, the whisky priest of Ford, Nichols and Fonda trudged through the film in a state of somnolent sanctimoniousness.

It was a year of noble martyrs and masochists – Verdoux, Ivan, Johnny McQueen in *Odd Man Out*, the children in *Shoeshine*, Aldo Fabrizi's persecuted patriarch in *To Live in Peace*, Maurice Chevalier's ageing matinee idol in *Man About Town*, Sam Levene's crucified Jew on the cross of anti-Semitism in *Crossfire*, John Garfield's morally anguished boxer in Robert Rossen's *Body and Soul*, Victor Mature's suffering stool-pigeon in Henry Hathaway's *Kiss of Death*, and, most forebodingly of all, Alf Kjellin's traumatized student in Alf Sjöberg's *Hets* (*Frenzy* or *Torment*) with a script by Ingmar Bergman. It was a year in which pain and torture and paranoia had finally overwhelmed the *film noir* – Anthony Mann's *T-Men*, Jacques Tourneur's *Out of the Past*, Robert Rossen's *Johnny O'Clock*, Robert Wise's *Born to Kill*, Jules Dassin's *Brute Force*, Byron Haskin's *I Walk Alone*, Robert Montgomery's *Ride the Pink Horse*, Irving Pichel's *They Won't Believe me* and Delmer Daves' *Dark Passage*. It was a year also in which Michael Powell and Emeric Pressburger were hailed for confronting the pathology of repression in the comely religious celibates of *Black Narcissus*. Against this background of spiritual and psychological disintegration, the glowingly pro-Catholic propaganda in *The Fugitive* seemed very naïve indeed. Even in 1947, it seemed unfair to stack the deck for the Catholic Church in any Latin American setting, however allegorical. What was paradoxical in the Greene novel became polemical in the Ford film, and what was dialectical became dogmatic. Worst of all, Mexico was neither Ireland nor the Old West, and despite the stylistic contributions of cinematographer Gabriel Figueroa and associate producer Emilio Fernandez, the Mexican characters in *The Fugitive* froze into a stone-faced stoicism more appropriate for a religious pageant than for a psychological drama. (Ford was later to experience a similar failure with the Indian characters in his nobly intentioned *Cheyenne Autumn.*)

Thus, *The Fugitive* shares a certain gloominess and half-baked ambitiousness with the more fashionable films of the late Forties; but the content simply isn't there. All the stock figures are seen so far from the outside that they become too prettily posed and expressively contorted: J. Carrol Naish's police informer crawling on the ground like a snake, Dolores Del Rio's Magdalene photographed with the shadowy serenity of a Madonna, Ward Bond's El Gringo outlaw posing before a Wanted Poster in a low-angle shot more appropriate for a Station of the Cross, and Fonda's pursued priest, his back to an endless wall, his face moodily impassive and ox-like in its spiritual obstinacy. It is more in the spatial transitions between compositions than in the interplay of characters that one senses Ford's grand design of interlocking narratives. Even so, Ford generally promises more visually than he can deliver dramatically. Hence, the shot in which the outlaw and the priest pass each other on the road, and move in opposite directions to an ultimately shared destiny, is too portentous for the skimpily allegorical resolution of this shared destiny as that of a Jesus and a Good Thief in a two-bit gunfight with the evil authorities. And when Ford reaches the heart of Greene's novel in the final confrontation between the priest and the atheist revolutionary, there are no dramatic sparks from the encounter. Armendariz is too much the solemn heavy, and Fonda too much the sullen martyr, cut off by casting from the rhythmic truths of his supposed people. Even the eye-popping Ford–Figueroa chiaroscuro compositions falsify Greene's grey relativism with an inappropriately black-and-white Manicheism. All in all, Ford's achievement in *The Fugitive* is more painterly than poetic, more for the eye than for the mind or heart.

4: 1948–1966: The Poet and Remberer of Things Past

Fort Apache (1948) took Ford further and deeper into the Old West than he had ever ventured before, but in the process it removed him from the stream of supposedly serious film history. The films Ford made between 1948 and 1966 seemed out of time in their own time. It was not that he stood still or that his work was unvarying. Quite the contrary: the last two decades of his career were his richest and most rewarding and most invigorating in that he became fully his own man. Indeed, the operative comparison is not with a Cecil B. DeMille or a Henry King, but rather with a Jean Renoir or a Carl Dreyer or a Kenji Mizoguchi. But to the critics of his time and even after, the late Ford appeared as a grizzled old prospector who lost his way out in Monument Valley.

From *Fort Apache* on, Ford's films seemed to have abandoned the Tradition of Quality for a Cult of Personality. Ford seemed to let everything hang out, and especially his boozy, misty-eyed Irishness. His casting was more casual than ever, and casting had never been his strongest point. The same old faces kept popping up year after year, film after film, most often in Western garb or military uniform. As Ford himself passed from his mid-fifties to his seventies, it became easier and easier for critics to write him off as an honoured has-been. He would be remembered, the conventional wisdom asserted, for *The Grapes of Wrath* and *The Informer*, and not much more. *Stagecoach*, perhaps, and *My Darling Clementine* might survive as genre studies. Of his post-1948 output, only *The Quiet Man* had any apparent claim on posterity, but more as pleasant entertainment than as expressive art. For the rest, the establishment critics lowered their heads in embarrassment and regret for a faded talent.

As a consequence, Ford's reputation sagged with everyone except a small coterie of his Hollywood colleagues and co-workers, and a bizarre succession of relatively esoteric critics. First were the *Sequence* and *Sight and Sound* generation of Lindsay Anderson, Gavin Lambert and Penelope Houston, against whom the New Cahierist critics of *Oxford Opinion* and *Movie* (notably Ian Cameron, Mark Shivas, Paul Mayersberg and Robin Wood) rebelled by declaring a preference for Sam Fuller over John Ford. Then in the early Sixties a two-man cabal of New York auteurists (the late Eugene Archer and myself) confounded the *Cahiers* line by placing John Ford on the same exalted level as Howard Hawks and Alfred Hitchcock. *Cahiers* itself finally re-evaluated Ford's stock in the mid-Sixties. But by then it was not nearly enough to say whether or not you liked Ford; you had to specify the key films and the richest period. Old Guard: *The Informer* and *The Grapes of Wrath* (1935–1940); Commitment School: *She Wore a Yellow Ribbon* and *Wagonmaster* (1949–1952); Auteurist School: *The Searchers* and *The Man Who Shot Liberty Valance* (1956–1966).

As always, however, the compleat Ford did not fit very conveniently into any of the cultish cubby-holes. No single theory could encompass both *The Sun Shines Bright* and *Mogambo*, or both *The Wings of Eagles* and *The Rising of the Moon*, or both *The Last Hurrah* and *Gideon of Scotland Yard*. Studio policies continued to exercise some influence on Ford's career in this period. Again, Ford seemed to fall into a pattern of personal atonement in such films as *Sergeant Rutledge* (towards the blacks), *Cheyenne Autumn* (towards the Indians) and *Seven Women* (towards the female of the species).

Viewed in tandem, *The Fugitive* and *Fort Apache* indicated a shift in Ford's sensibility from the shadowy world of Dudley Nichols to the sunlit world of Frank S. Nugent, from socially conscious allegory to crowd-pleasing adventure, and from the lies of art to the half-truths of legend. The very plot of *Fort Apache* suggested a conscious shift in the casting of the Ford hero from Henry Fonda, the star of Ford's Quality Period, to John Wayne, the star of the director's Personality Period. It was the first and last time Fonda and Wayne appeared together in a Ford film, Fonda as a Custer-like martinet of a colonel and Wayne as a wily Indian fighter. The iconographical tension alone makes *Fort Apache* one of Ford's most absorbing

125

entertainments, but there is much more as well, and in some areas much too much. The casting of Shirley Temple as Philadelphia Thursday, the coyly flirtatious daughter of Lt.-Col. Thursday (Henry Fonda) marked the reunion of Ford with his child star of *Wee Willie Winkie*. That Miss Temple's grown-up career had not flourished probably only strengthened Ford's resolve to employ her. But if Miss Temple's disastrously discordant performance could be chalked off to Auld Lang Syne, John Agar's pretty-boy petulance as her young West Point suitor could only be explained as a misguided effort to exploit the Temple–Agar marriage in real life. As it was, the Temple–Agar subplot seemed so interminable that the extraordinary virtues of the main plot were almost completely overlooked. The set pieces are among Ford's most memorable: the Grand March at the Enlisted Men's Ball; the women's farewell to the men going off to war; and the Apache massacre of the Seventh Cavalry.

Unfortunately, *Fort Apache* was released at a time when Hollywood was afflicted with realistic *rigor mortis*. Critics of the period lacked the language to describe and evaluate myth and romance. Problems and polemics were the order of the day, and *Fort Apache* seemed to have nothing new to say. The film's attitudes towards Indians, women and military discipline seemed either conventional or conservative. Indeed, the final eulogy of John Wayne's Captain Kirby York for his fallen Custer-like commander, Henry Fonda's Colonel Thursday, tends to glorify command decisions to the point of incompetence and even insanity. Moreover, Ford seemed unduly sentimental in healing the old wounds incurred in the Civil War by proud soldiers on both sides. Hence, much of the tension between the Fonda and Wayne characters is generated by a series of Yankee-versus-Reb insult routines in which Fonda's officious nastiness is allowed to play against Wayne's submissive exasperation. But there is no corresponding ideological tension between the two officers. What unites them – the Seventh Cavalry rather than the Union – is much stronger than what has divided them in the past largely through an accident of geography.

The American cinema has generally sentimentalized the Southern (or American Trojan) position in the Civil War while reserving the right to be critical of the victorious Northern (or American Greek) forces. Never, for example, was there a kind word for General Sherman, the master strategist of total war, and seldom an under-

Fort Apache: Manifest Destiny

standing word for John Brown, the ill-fated abolitionist who made the mistake of practising a premature emancipation of the slaves. The movie studios regarded the South as a distinct region with very deep and lingering emotions about the Civil War. By contrast, the North was credited with sufficient historical detachment to forgive and forget, and even to identify with the romantic plight of the defeated Southland. Ford's films did not always take the Southern point of view. Indeed, John Wayne himself played Sherman and Henry (Harry) Morgan played Grant in Ford's Civil War episode in MGM's Cinerama grab-bag demonstration, *How the West Was Won* (1962). *The Horse Soldiers* (1959) celebrated the feats of arms of a marauding Union cavalry unit far behind the Confederate lines in 1863, and Ford provided a sympathetic portrait of General Philip Sheridan by J. Carrol Naish in *Rio Grande* (1950), and of Grant as President by Edward G. Robinson in *Cheyenne Autumn.*

Still, Ford preferred to accept history and even legend as it was written rather than revise it in a radical or derisive spirit. Why are the Indians on the warpath from *Fort Apache* to *Cheyenne Autumn*? Not, according to Ford, because of American Imperialism or White Racism or Manifest Destiny, but because of the derelictions of the Indian Ring, 'the most corrupt band of politicians in our nation's history'; graft and corruption on the local level rather than greed and conquest on the national level. Thus, the Indian remains the Other in American history and mythology to the end of Ford's career. Even in the moderately revisionist *Cheyenne Autumn*, the Indians provide little more than an occasion for their conquerors to be merciful and belatedly virtuous. One of Ford's most tendentious films, *Cheyenne Autumn* comes to life only momentarily when the focus shifts from the nobly but opaquely suffering Indians to the wild frontier slapstick of Wyatt Earp (James Stewart) and Doc Holliday (Arthur Kennedy) as they debunk anti-Indian hysteria. One must, however, distinguish between reasons and excuses. Critics who claim to dislike Ford because of the implicit political positions of his Westerns are generally not all that enthusiastic about the genre itself. Certainly, the aggressively anti-heroic Westerns of the Sixties and Seventies have not provided a validly artistic alternative to Ford's vision of the region and the period. It is almost as if the ideology comes wrapped up in the genre so that the racism can never be dissociated from the romance.

128

Another excess of *Fort Apache* was its boisterous Irishness, particularly the boozy, brutish braggadocio of Victor McLaglen's Sergeant Mulcahy. McLaglen had long since earned his spurs with Ford as a brawling giant, but as he grew older, his performances began to lose every semblance of substance and he degenerated into the most tedious of comedy reliefs. None the less, Ford stayed with McLaglen through *She Wore a Yellow Ribbon, Rio Grande* and *The Quiet Man*, and even managed to modulate his performances by suggesting the blubbering baby under the overgrown id. A standard Ford gambit with McLaglen was the taming of the giant by a little wisp of a woman after he had virtually demolished a tavern along with all its muscularly male occupants. Thus was the Irish-Catholic Caliban calmed and conquered by the Madonna.

Ford increasingly indulged his sociologically distorted Irishness to the end of his career. The South, the West, the Past all swirled together in an Irish stew of the most indulgent sentimentality. The poet was often too garrulous and too gregarious for the good of his material. The Ford–Nugent adaptation of Frank O'Connor's *The Last Hurrah* lost much of the novel's biting humour by too tenderly caressing the roguish Boston Irish politicos as they faded from the scene. Ford lacked the sharp eye for satirical detail of a Preston Sturges or a Billy Wilder. Sturges, especially, would have been ideal not only for *The Last Hurrah*, but also for *When Willie Comes Marching Home*, a very feeble and outdated effort by Ford to cash in on the 1944 success of Sturges' *Hail the Conquering Hero*.

Except for *The Whole Town's Talking* back in the mid-Thirties, Ford's touch had always been too heavy, and his timing too clumsy, for the rigorous demands of farce comedy. Also, his visual style had always been too elegantly premeditated and ceremonial for the sudden jolts of iconoclastic indiscretion. Ford's films are never to be laughed at in any sense. The seemingly interminable shouting matches of a Dan Dailey and a James Cagney in *What Price Glory?*, or of a Dan Dailey and a William Demarest in *When Willie Comes Marching Home*, or of a John Wayne and a Lee Marvin in *Donovan's Reef*, are not so much to be enjoyed as to be endured until Ford can lead us into the beating heart of the film. In *What Price Glory?* it is the moment in which Corinne Calvet's Charmaine comes down the stairs bathed in a filter like the Lady of Shalott and James

The Last Hurrah: (Spencer Tracy)

Cagney's Captain Flagg gazes at her as he recites his litany of the fighting man. It is the moment also in which Dan Dailey's hapless Willie bids adieu to Corinne Calvet's Yvonne of the French Resistance, and the scene takes on the poignant lilt of romance despite the satirical premise of the plot. To appreciate Ford fully, one must learn to wait very patiently for his emotional epiphanies. In fact, the broadness of his humour is the price we must pay for the depth of his feelings.

There are of course many other sides to the Irishness of John Ford besides the blustering and blubbering of Victor McLaglen and the blithering and blathering of Barry Fitzgerald. Actors like James Cagney (*What Price Glory?*) and Spencer Tracy (*The Last Hurrah*) transcend their Irishness even for Ford. Ironically, one of the problems with Tracy in *The Last Hurrah* is that he seems more to tower over his milieu than to rise out of it, and it is only when he takes to his deathbed that the film springs to emotional life, particularly with his compassionate leave-taking of his wastrel son, a mediocre prodigal (Arthur Walsh).

In many ways, *The Last Hurrah* seems in retrospect to have been one long rehearsal for Ford's own last farewell. None of his later films seems so totally orchestrated to the cadences of a funeral march. The casting resembled a resurrection of such gallant luminaries as Pat O'Brien, Basil Rathbone, James Gleason, John Carradine, Ricardo Cortez, Frank Albertson, Wallace Ford, Frank

130

McHugh, Edmund Lowe, Dan Borzage and most memorably of all Ed Brophy's Ditto Boland, the mournful Dopey of Skeffington's solicitous Seven Dwarfs in their processional up the stairs to the death bed on which the snow white hair of Skeffington rests in a state of emotional enchantment. None the less, Ford could be reasonably criticized for having lacked the energy and temperament to give *The Last Hurrah* the comic zip it deserved. The modern urban setting seems too well-scrubbed and orderly to suggest a contemporary city, and Jeffrey Hunter's callow young reporter seems to belong more on an open range than in the teeming streets. But though Ford was not truly in his element, the death of Skeffington remains one of his noblest and most soul-searching achievements.

Although Ford's Irishness is implicit in all his work, the Irishness is virtually institutionalized in three of his late films – *The Quiet Man* (1952), *The Long Gray Line* (1955) and *The Rising of the Moon* (1957). *Young Cassidy* (1965) would have been a fourth, but Ford's ill-health prevented him from shooting more than a scene or two from what would have been his penultimate film. Jack Cardiff completed this romantic treatment of Sean O'Casey's early struggles against Irish Philistinism, and the result was creditable though not unduly compelling. Still, the coupling of Ford with O'Casey does not seem politically consistent with the couplings of Ford with Wayne, Bond and McLaglen.

The Quiet Man earned Ford his last Oscar for direction. 1952 had seemed a strange year to the Motion Picture Academy, with the members unable to decide between *The Quiet Man*, Fred Zinnemann's super-allegory *High Noon*, and Cecil B. DeMille's super-spectacle *The Greatest Show on Earth*. In the end the Academy hedged its bets by honouring *High Noon* with an award to Gary Cooper as best actor, *The Quiet Man* with a fourth nod to Ford, and then wound up the evening on a cynically ecumenical note by naming *The Greatest Show on Earth* best picture. The New York Film Critics that year had gone whole-hog for *High Noon* as best picture, and Fred Zinnemann as best director, but for best actor they cited Ralph Richardson in David Lean's *The Sound Barrier* (not to mention, which the critics did not, Richardson's equally sterling portrayal in Carol Reed's *Outcast of the Islands*). No one saw fit to commemorate Charles Chaplin's extraordinary elegy in *Limelight*, but Chaplin was considered washed up by the wiseacres on both coasts, and Ford, though not as completely written off as Chaplin, was none the less dismissed as a quaint relic of bygone days.

All in all, the heavy-thinking Fifties were not (in America, at least) a period of auteurist retrospection, and thus *The Quiet Man* was tolerated, if at all, less as a profoundly Fordian testament than as a poetical travel folder. In Britain and in France, however, critical judgments were more thoughtful. The *Sequence-Sight and Sound* School of Personal Commitment responded to *The Quiet Man* for its director's stylistic quirks and emotional effusions. Ford's joyous submission to the fateful forces of Nature may have seemed to the British not only other-worldly, but also old-worldly. In France, *The Quiet Man* appealed to that generous spirit of ethnographic inquiry which has characterized the French temperament from Montaigne to Lévi-Strauss. Also, the iconographical associations of John Wayne and Maureen O'Hara were not culturally as unfashionable in Paris as in New York and Hollywood. Indeed, Wayne himself did not seem to realize his problems with the taste-makers of the time when he remarked jokingly to Cooper at the Oscar ceremonies that he wished his own agent could get him parts as good as Cooper's in *High Noon*. Ironically, Wayne's performance in *The Quiet Man* is more forceful and less mannered than Cooper's in *High Noon*, and his part is far less contrived, rhetorical and pretentious. The Wayne–Cooper comparison may be but a footnote to film history, but it is crucial to an understanding of Ford's declining reputation through the Fifties.

Though *The Quiet Man* was lovingly underrated in its own time, it does not emerge in retrospect as one of Ford's relaxed masterpieces on the level, say, of *Wagonmaster* or *The Searchers* or *Wings of Eagles* or *The Man Who Shot Liberty Valance*. In its measured pacing and lazy beauty, it is perhaps closer to such overformalized achievements as *She Wore a Yellow Ribbon, The Sun Shines Bright* and *The Long Gray Line*. Curiously, one must penetrate beneath the superficial prettiness of *The Quiet Man* to perceive its visual fusion of the human and the natural in an oppressive order. From the first moment that John Wayne's Sean Thornton falls under the spell of the landscape and lethargy of Ireland, he seems enmeshed in a dialectical conflict between the warm browns and reds of carnal passion and the cold blues and greens of Catholic protocol. In this context, Maureen O'Hara's flaming red hair is as much a force of nature as a figure of

The Quiet Man: the horse race; and (*below*) matchmaker and bride (Barry Fitzgerald, Maureen O'Hara)

style. Never before or after was Ford's sensuality so studied. The wind whips a long skirt against a girl's rigid legs with a baroque sweep and tension worthy almost of an El Greco, and the fierce rain reveals the straining flesh of the two lovers against the clinging fabrics of convention and repression.

All round the edges of this idyll of lovers is a community of congenital busybodies, the most conspicuous of whom is Barry Fitzgerald's meddlesome matchmaker and tippler, Michaeleen Oge Flynn. Indeed, the biggest laugh in the movie is provided by the zonked expression on Fitzgerald's face when he sees the broken bed ('Impetuous – Homeric') in the Wayne–O'Hara cottage. Wayne had

The Quiet Man: bringing home the bride (O'Hara and Wayne)

actually thrown O'Hara on the bed more in anger than in passion, and the marriage had not actually been consummated, and thus the audience laughed as much at knowing something that Fitzgerald did not know as at the evil thoughts in his mind. This does not really make the movie coy in the customarily prurient manner of Hollywood hypocrisy, but there is something dispiriting in the very success of the gag just the same. What it means is that we can laugh uproariously only before the couple has crossed the great divide of copulation. Afterwards, the business of living – and dying – will begin, and the laughter will become muted in the sweet sadness of trying to remember.

Especially cyclical and communal in *The Quiet Man* are the celebrated set pieces of the horse race (which is more a tour of the elemental Irish landscape and seascape) and the Wayne–McLaglen donnybrook (which we see mostly through the eyes and enthusiasm of the villagers). It is never a question of the race being to the swift, and the fight to the strong. Both contests are photographed in the circular forms of communion rather than in the angular forms of competition. As the horsemen ride from the sod to the sea and back, we neither know nor care about the order of finish. There is no subjective intercutting of close-ups against faked process backgrounds to mar the majestic indifference of Ford's cosmic long shots to the immediate issues of the race. Indeed, there are no issues; there is only the Emerald Isle as a feudal sanctuary to which rich and even not-so-rich Irish-Americans can escape in their flight from America's clamorous competitiveness. (Scotland serves very much the same purpose in *Brigadoon* and *I Know Where I'm Going*.) And, of course, *The Quiet Man* represents very much a retreat into the pastoral and horse-driven past. It is not for Ford to invoke on this festive occasion the spectres of poverty, bigotry, ignorance, inequality and injustice.

Curiously, *The Quiet Man* was very much ahead of its time in staging a donnybrook over a bride's dowry. Molly Haskell discusses Ford's startlingly feminist insight in *From Reverence to Rape: The Treatment of Women in the Movies*:

The theme becomes the explicit subject of one of John Ford's loveliest (and from this point of view, most surprising) films, *The Quiet Man*. In marrying John Wayne, the American who has come back to live in Ireland, Maureen O'Hara's redhead Irish firebrand insists on recovering her dowry from her father: a £350 'fortune' and her furniture. Wayne is indignant. In characteristic American fashion, he feels his masculinity and ability to provide for her impugned, until she finally makes him understand that it isn't the money, but what it stands for: the dowry and furniture are her identity, her independence. The furniture, particularly, is part of her personality – like a maiden name – and the money enables her not to be completely dependent on her husband and 'absorbed' by him. When she finally does recover the money, she throws it into a furnace.

There is also in the donnybrook an acting out of the courtly convention by which a man is obligated to fight for the woman of his choice. This is the comic premise of Ingmar Bergman's *Lesson in Love*, one of his most enchanting comedies. It is not surprising that Europeans, with their more cultivated insight into archetypes, should be more responsive to the mythological resonance of *The Quiet Man*. By contrast, the American reaction to *The Quiet Man* has tended to be one of uncomplicated amusement.

The Long Gray Line would seem at first glance to belong more to Ford's Army testimonials than to his Irish testaments. The rows upon rows of marching West Point cadets in tilted Cinemascope seemed in 1955 to belong to an earlier era. At one point in the proceedings Tyrone Power's Martin Maher is scolded by his gruff Irish father (Donald Crisp) for betting on the Army against Notre Dame ('Our Lady'), even though the movie is about Martin Maher's half century of devoted service to the Military Academy. Ford's hapless hero loses the bet to his father, and almost everything else one can lose in a lifetime. In the early part of the film, Power takes pratfalls in every athletic event he attempts to play or coach. Ford's slapstick is more strained than ever, and Power's inexpressive earnestness does not help. Of all the good-looking, no-acting male stars of the Thirties and Forties, Power was the least tainted by any trace of professional expertise. Unlike Dick Powell and Robert Taylor, Power did not toughen and improve with age. His alternating expressions of fatuousness and petulance simply became puffier and less photogenic. It is somehow typical of Ford that he should have escaped Power when they were both under contract at Fox, and when Fonda was the class actor on the Fox lot. The critics were important to Ford back then. But by 1955 Ford was marching to the music of a different drum, and Power's very inadequacy seemed perfect for Ford's deification of the quintessential loser. Hence, most people's prevailing impression of *The Long Gray Line* as an interminable series of recruiting posters is superficial and misleading.

What is generally overlooked in the film is its peculiar ambivalence about its thoroughly mediocre protagonist. Time and again, family situations are charged with more regard than respect. No one ever really counts on Marty Maher for any sensitivity or perception. His only virtues are his awesome patience and his ox-like devotion to duty. When his wife (Maureen O'Hara) loses her baby and the capacity ever to have another, our loser bears up well under the blow, but then there is a bit of Mr Chips in his attitude to the succeeding classes of cadets. As long as they keep coming, he will never be childless. What he is never able to understand is his wife's spiritual adoption of one of the cadets as a surrogate son, an attachment so strong that she never forgives her husband for persuading the cadet to go off to war. Ford's lingering shot of Maureen O'Hara gazing

The Long Gray Line: Tyrone Power, Maureen O'Hara

after her departed surrogate son is one of the most powerful images of loss in the Ford *oeuvre*.

Bitterness, loss and defeat figure so strongly in the main characterizations of *The Long Gray Line* that the consolatory conformism of the Academy itself seems grotesquely out of key. Hence, the ghostly ending in which Power's aged retainer 'sees' the phantoms of all his lost loved ones does not work as it did in *How Green Was My Valley*. For one thing, the ridiculous pomp and ceremony of a West Point graduation seems an inappropriate occasion for a visitation from the dear departed. Also, Power is not up to the histrionic challenges of this world, much less of the next. None the less, *The Long Gray Line* impinges upon some of Ford's deepest feelings, particularly in that extraordinarily magical moment when Power opens the door to his dining room, and sees his family fresh from Ireland matter-of-factly eating their dinner. They ignore his amazed expression as they calmly finish their meal. Then the father rises, and blesses their table and their adopted country, and the old order of *The Quiet Man* is translated in the new land. It is a scene with such uncanny reverberations that it stays in the mind long after the endlessly marching men have been mercifully forgotten.

The Rising of the Moon was adapted by Frank S. Nugent from a short story, *The Majesty of the Law* by Frank O'Connor, and two short plays, *A Minute's Wait* by Michael J. McHugh, and *The Rising of the Moon* by Lady Gregory. But whereas *The Long Voyage Home*, adapted from several short Eugene O'Neill plays, had been fused by Dudley Nichols into a single screenplay, *The Rising of the Moon* was written and filmed as a collection of short, unrelated episodes. For various reasons the period from the late Forties through the Fifties seemed more amenable than any period before or since to the so-called anthology or episode film.

The commercial taboo against the short fictional film has generally followed the same pattern of justification as the commercial taboo in publishing against the short story or the collection of short stories. Of course, any commercial taboo tends to become self-fulfilling. Still, the movie moguls were pleasantly surprised with the popular and critical success of the three Somerset Maugham packets: *Quartet* (1949), *Trio* (1950) and *Encore* (1952). What made the Maugham movies unusual was their frank and unabashed tribute to the writer as their sole *raison d'être*. Maugham himself served as the master of ceremonies, and there was no link between one episode and another, unlike such earlier American quasi-anthology films as *If I Had a Million* and *Tales of Manhattan*, themselves turgid imitations of René Clair's *Le Million*. In each instance, narrative segments were linked together with more or less ingenuity either to expose some universal vice or to exhibit an assemblage of stars in cameo parts, and sometimes both. The literary models were usually comic in tone and promise (Chaucer, Boccaccio, Jonson, Labiche, Feydeau *et al.*), but on the screen the mood of anthology films tended more often than not to be mixed.

By contrast, John Ford's conception in *The Rising of the Moon* seems institutionally Irish with a vengeance. The three episodes ranged from the incomprehensible (with Cyril Cusack and Noel Purcell virtually burying their lines under thick brogues), to the insubstantial (*Quiet Man* shenanigans at a village railway station) and the ineffable (Ford's meditation in tilted Cinemascope on Lady Gregory's one-act vision of Ireland's tragic awakening to her own destiny). Ford seems somewhat more detached from the Ireland of *The Rising of the Moon* than he was from the Ireland of *The Quiet Man*. In the casting, for example, he is completely cut off from his stock company – Wayne, O'Hara, McLaglen, Bond. Hence, such noted Abbey players as Eileen Crowe and Jack McGowran are more prominent here than they were in the background of *The Quiet Man*.

'Institutionally Irish with a vengeance': *The Rising of the Moon*

(A double-edged legend has grown up about the later Ford's alleged preference for raw, unschooled performers who could grunt out their lines on the first take. Ford's ease with the most anarchic of Abbey players, and with Mildred Natwick, one of the American theatre's most expert comediennes, should lay *that* legend to rest.)

Ultimately, it is Ireland's very strangeness that Ford is celebrating in *The Rising of the Moon*, as his characters teeter on the very thin line between steadfastness and stubbornness, patience and procrastination, courage and bombast. Each episode serves a deceptively simple anecdote. In the first the law comes calling upon a proud, obsessively traditional landowner, who surrenders to the majesty of that law, a majesty epitomized not so much by the soft-spoken lawman himself as by the towering trees and majestic landscape of the lawman's jurisdiction. In the second episode a train pulls into a village station for 'a minute's wait', and stays the length of an ethnographic vignette on dawdling village life. If one has ever gnashed one's teeth on Irish folk humour, one must prepare to gnash them here. There is the strapping colleen who gleefully kisses a boy, and then just as gleefully slaps his face to preserve the moral hypocrisy of her heritage. There is the jovial apotheosis of provincial perverseness, and the joyful indulgence of alcoholism as a lyrical extension of leprechaunism, and, almost in passing, an ethnic smugness towards the English. As in *The Quiet Man*, there is from Old Albion a stock character of impenetrable stuffiness who never gets into the spirit of the Irish frolics around him.

Ford's attitude towards the English has always been one of amused condescension rather than of anger or contempt. Thus it is more the clumsiness of the caricature than its savagery which is artistically objectionable. The ridiculously jaunty English flier in *The Lost Patrol* remains one of Ford's most egregious expressions of his attitude towards the English aristocracy, but more often Ford tended to trot out the old stiff-upper-lip clichés about the English with an air of directorial absent-mindedness, never looking beneath the stereotype for the subterranean feelings of individuals. With the English, Ford's mystical poetry turns into mechanical prose. He observes, but he does not intervene.

It is this passive, distanced quality, which makes *Gideon of Scotland Yard* one of Ford's most peculiar projects in his late period. From the opening shot of Jack Hawkins' nightmarish confrontation with a slowly dollying camera (an effect which is more hallucinatory in colour prints of the film than in the black-and-white version in general release) to the closing shot of Hawkins' bemused mini-triumph over an overly scrupulous son-in-law to be, Ford has packed more incident into one feature film than in to any five of his other films. He seems to be mocking not only the English but also the nouveau-Scotland Yard genre of which *Gideon's Day* by J. J. Marric (a pseudonym for John Creasey) was a typical example. Whereas Ford's Irish tend to be indolent and dilatory, his English are hustling and bustling in their bumbling manner, with periodic pauses for their tepid tea and beastly buns, and then back to the treadmill of their eccentrically formalized routines. Ford plays up the comedy and the satire at the expense of the more sombre Simenonism of the genre itself, but his gallery of English and Irish actors somehow become extraordinarily vivid on the fly, as it were, as if they could have taken off to loftier realms of mood and insight if Ford had responded to them with a fraction of the feeling he devotes to Denis O'Dea's police sergeant and Eileen Crowe's bed-warming and conscience-stirring wife in the third episode of *The Rising of the Moon*. With Ford it is truly a question of accepting an inescapable connection between the level of his artistic expression and the intensity of his emotional commitment; and the last episode in *The Rising of the Moon*, with its conjugal epiphany of a policeman-turned-patriot and his prideful Penelope's weaving her tapestry of tact, becomes one of the most exquisite achievements of Ford's career.

It was in the period of *The Rising of the Moon*, however, that Ford's critical standing seemed to be at its lowest ebb. The industry eyed him rather dubiously for having presumed to tamper with a certified Broadway success like *Mister Roberts*, a film on which he was replaced (because of illness) by Mervyn LeRoy, and the film which caused an irrevocable break with Henry Fonda (and reportedly a fistfight as well). He was betwixt and between the British cultists of commitment (too reactionary in content) and the British cultists of Cahierism (too conservative in form). His spectacles never attained the critical cachet of David Lean's *The Bridge on the River Kwai* or even William Wyler's *Ben Hur*, and his adaptation to the Cinemascope screen was regarded as conspicuously maladroit. At the time there were two schools of thought on Cinemascope, and Ford seemed to have flunked in both. The classicists, who considered the 2·35 to 1 screen ratio hopelessly grotesque for any subject apart from a slithering snake, condemned Ford for using Cinemascope at all. Ford himself seemed to mock the pretensions of the process with a prolonged tilting of his camera in both *The Long Gray Line* and *The Rising of the Moon*. For the modernists, however, his rigid response to the challenge of wide screen was dismissed as so much formal foot-dragging. The neurotically contorted compositions of Elia Kazan's *East of Eden* and Nicholas Ray's *Rebel Without a Cause* were widely hailed as more creative uses of Cinemascope, and abroad Max Ophüls's *Lola Montès* influenced a whole generation of French *cinéastes* in the direction of the wide screen.

If Ford could be charged with indifference towards Cinemascope, he could be charged with downright intransigence towards the Cinerama process employed in *How the West Was Won*. From its first promotional film (*This is Cinerama*) in 1952, Cinerama, like Cinemascope, was hailed as the film industry's technological answer to the commercial challenge of television, just as the Warners Vitaphone had been heralded as the industry's answer to radio a generation before. About all the Cinerama process was good for were roller-coaster rides and aerial travelogues, and even these carnival effects depended too much on the viewer's seat location. Critics with choice sight-lines at previews could afford to be indulgent, but the paying customer, stuck on one side or too far to the front or back, risked optical migraine. Even under the best viewing conditions, Cinerama was less than a mixed blessing. After ten years and five pilot films, the Cinerama screen was still afflicted by jiggling lines between the three separately projected panels; the stereophonic sound was still grotesquely inappropriate for any setting more intimate than the Grand Canyon; and the horizon line still curved upwards around the edges. When experienced directors like John Ford, Henry Hathaway and George Marshall were unable to overcome the technical problems of the process, it was clearly time to junk the process.

Otherwise, the acting of an 'all-star' cast in *How the West Was Won* is too perfunctory, the scenario too diffuse, the spectacle too contrived, for any serious analysis. What remains of interest is how three directors diverged stylistically on a doomed stunt assignment. Henry Hathaway blithely treats the first half of the film – the rivers and valleys portion – as if Cinerama had never been invented,

How the West Was Won

allowing the process' jiggling lines to part rivers and rapids like the Red Sea of Moses' time. On land he sets up compositions with trees over the lines, but all this accomplishes is a bizarre folding and creasing of a real tree as if it were made of mouldy papier-mâché. An action director of the old school, Hathaway is more effective with a smashing train robbery than with static compositions of pioneers clumsily grouped at their camp sites.

When John Ford takes command of the relatively brief Civil War sequences, he changes the mood of the film from light adventure to heart-rending nostalgia. Ford exploits triptych compositions and studio lighting to conceal the deficiencies of Cinerama. Whether he is showing a farm boy going off to war on a lonely road or a surgeon's blood-drenched operating table at Shiloh, the dominant images run vertically down the centre of the middle panel. To block out the jiggling lines Ford employs not sunlit trees but studio-lit fence posts with shadowed perspective. A farewell scene is staged on the extreme right of the screen with a house blocking out the rest, and two brothers actually shake hands across the jiggling line as if to exorcize it with fraternal feeling.

George Marshall brought nothing to the project but his formless amiability and shaggy-dog sensibility. His sequences fell into place with neither Ford's spirituality nor Hathaway's physicality, but they did at least fall into place, as befitted the director of that version of *Destry Rides Again* with James Stewart and Marlene Dietrich, and that memorable comedy sleeper of the Forties, *Murder, He Says*, and a couple of hundred other entertainments with more charm than ambition. For the new movie–movie-oriented critics in Paris, London and New York, the problem with Ford was that he seemed to reek of the wrong kind of formal ambition in that his films appeared to yearn to be more than flicks. By this funky standard, Ford's contribution to *How the West Was Won* was considered markedly inferior to Hathaway's and Marshall's. Ironically, Ford's mere involvement in *How the West Was Won* marked him as hopelessly frivolous in the eyes of the American critical establishment.

Through the late Forties and early Fifties Ford strengthened the impression that he was standing still by turning out no fewer than four remakes of earlier movies. *Three Godfathers* (1948) was a remake of his own *Marked Men* (1919), itself remade in the intervening years by William Wyler (*Hell's Heroes*, 1930) and Richard Boleslavski (*Three Godfathers*, 1936). *What Price Glory?* was an elegant reprise of Raoul Walsh's earthier 1926 movie from the play by Maxwell Anderson and Laurence Stallings. *The Sun Shines Bright* (1953) was an elaboration of the folk materials of Ford's own *Judge Priest* (1934), and *Mogambo* a relatively 'straight' remake of Victor Fleming's zesty 1932 entertainment, *Red Dust*. None of these remakes, however, could be considered routine or mechanical. In each instance, Ford altered the tone, and enlarged the scope of the original. Indeed, the remakes cannot be properly or adequately appreciated unless one is thoroughly familiar with the earlier treatments of the same basic anecdotal material. It is not a question of better or worse, or more or less original, but rather of a shift in stylistic and thematic emphasis.

Three Godfathers tends to be somewhat of an embarrassment even to Ford's most ardent admirers. The pulpy Peter B. Kyne plot about three desert desperadoes performing like the Magi when confronted with a dying mother and her new-born babe was no longer viable in 1949. Worse, the film superimposed Ford's sentimental religiosity on the behavioural realism of his late Westerns. It was as if *The Fugitive* had wandered into *Fort Apache*, and the result is neither one thing nor the other, since *Three Godfathers* is too realistic for allegory and too ritualistic for adventure. From the very beginning Ford seems determined to dawdle over details as if he wanted to postpone his Passion Play at all costs. Hence, badman John Wayne and lawman Ward Bond spend an unconscionable amount of time on the whimsical possibilities of Bond's being named 'B. Sweet' in a he-man setting. By the time Wayne and his confederates (Harry Carey, Jr. and Pedro Armendariz) have finished laughing, and Bond's sheriff has finished thumbing over the Wanted circulars, and the badmen finish robbing the bank, and the sheriff finishes posting shotgun sentries along the railroad tracks, the audience is left with no clue to the ultimate shape or size of the story. Mildred Natwick's dying mother seems oddly intrusive, and her prairie Christ of a child seems unduly portentous. But the movie goes on and on until Wayne staggers into town on Christmas Day, the sole survivor of the three Magi, with his precious charge; and then, surprisingly, it tapers off into a leisurely resolution of the plot, and a complete slackening of all tension. *Three Godfathers* is unmistakably Fordian in its parts, but as a whole it is distractingly inconsistent in mood and tempo.

By contrast, *The Sun Shines Bright* seems to be everything Ford wanted it to be as a rigorously controlled and unified work of art. Its pacing has much of the grave deliberation of Dreyer's late films, especially *Gertrud*, and slow Ford is almost as hard on the average audience as slow Dreyer. Indeed, *The Sun Shines Bright* was everything an American movie was not supposed to be in 1954, a year in which fashion smiled on the tortured social consciousness of the Kazan–Schulberg *On the Waterfront* and the nagging problem drama of the Seaton–Odets *The Country Girl*. Not only did *The Sun Shines Bright* hearken to the soft murmurs of a reconstructed Kentucky town in 1905; it did so with a tin ear for rustic vaudeville in defiance of the new religion of Method mumbling. The heroes were humourlessly heroic, and the villains unvaryingly villainous. Virtue was rewarded and treachery punished just before the final chorus of 'My Old Kentucky Home'. Ford's set piece is a funeral procession for a prostitute, a movement which in its maddening slowness across the screen cuts like a dull blade across the social fabric of the town, separating the disapproving Yankee Methodist Temperance forces from the more amiable and more sentimental Southern Baptist Corn Liquor forces to which Judge Priest (Charles Winninger) owes his high office. This doctrinal division is almost the folksy equivalent of Dreyer's dialectical conflict between the God of Love and the God of Fear in *Ordet*.

In its celebration of communal feelings, *The Sun Shines Bright* followed immediately on the heels of *The Quiet Man*, but whereas the painted world of *The Quiet Man* seemed enchanted, the bleached world of *The Sun Shines Bright* seemed embalmed. Its feelings, like its plot devices, are not so much remembered as they are preserved. As a work of art, *The Sun Shines Bright* is more fully articulated and shaped than *Judge Priest* was back in Ford's contract days at Fox in the Thirties. But in doing it right the second time, Ford succeeded only in cutting himself off completely from Fifties' audiences in America. Not surprisingly, there was a small cult following for the film in Britain; not surprisingly because Ford's high artistic reputation lingered much longer abroad than it did at home.

The basic problem with *The Sun Shines Bright* today, however, is not its lack of commercial success and theatrical distribution in 1953 and 1954, but rather that it seems hermetically sealed off from the realities of its time. From an auteurist standpoint, the film is 100-proof Ford. Every shot, every frame is a testament to a lifetime of film-making and feeling. And in the central role of Judge Priest, Charles Winninger, the consummate Captain Andy of *Showboat*, was a considerably more expert actor than Will Rogers, no more than an eccentrically cadenced personality performer in his own time. Still, Rogers was more affecting than Winninger when it came to suggesting remembrance of things past. Whereas Rogers evoked a young man who had grown old, Winninger evoked a sterling character actor who had been born middle-aged. In a sense, Winninger's more polished professionalism made him seem more self-satisfied and less vulnerable than the shambling Rogers. Similarly, *The Sun Shines Bright* emerges as the kind of project that might have been better tossed off as a studio assignment than toiled over as a labour of love.

In terms of studio aesthetics, *The Sun Shines Bright* marked

The Sun Shines Bright: remembrance of things past (Charles Winninger, Russell Simpson)

Ford's last association with Republic, a low-grade studio memorialized in the campy precincts of Gore Vidalville by Vera Hruba Ralston, the wife and perennial protégé of Republic's President, Herbert Yates. From 1941 to 1958 Miss Ralston made twenty-six indescribably inane pictures, all for Republic. Paradoxically, Republic also participated in several very arty (though inexpensive) auteurist projects in this period. In addition to Ford's *Rio Grande*, *The Quiet Man* and *The Sun Shines Bright*, such strange conceits as Ben Hecht's *Spectre of the Rose*, Fritz Lang's *House by the River*, Nicholas Ray's *Johnny Guitar*, and Orson Welles' *Macbeth* were gathered under the moth-eaten wings of the Republic eagle in the clearest case ever of studio schizophrenia.

The Sun Shines Bright marked Ford's last association also with Stepin' Fetchit and Clarence Muse, two unfortunate emblems of Hollywood's racist caricature of blacks. Ford saw Fetchit and Muse as old companions on the back lot, but civil rights spokesmen saw them as shameful symbols of a discredited past. It was rumoured that Ford's conception of *Pinky*, a project taken over by Elia Kazan after Ford's illness, had been hopelessly paternalist and condescending to the Negro characters. From 1949 on Hollywood went through the motions of emancipating itself from its old racial taboos with a series of race-oriented melodramas – *Home of the Brave, Lost Boundaries, Pinky, No Way Out* and *Intruder in the Dust*. For the most part, however, the Negro performer was caught in a double bind. He was

147

denied the old stereotyped roles in the name of racial equality, and he was denied the more glamorous roles of the white world in the name of sociological realism. In the Fifties and early Sixties, Hollywood was not quite ready even for Sidney Poitier riding the New Haven to work every morning as the man in the grey flannel suit on his way to his Wall Street office. Indeed, it was still the rule for characters 'passing' as white to be played by certified Caucasian players such as Jeanne Crain (*Pinky*), and Mel Ferrer and Beatrice Pearson (*Lost Boundaries*). Shades of Jim Crow blackface minstrelsy! In this regard, James Earl Jones tells the story of a casting call for black actors to play an elevator operator in Elia Kazan's *A Face in the Crowd* (1957). Every black actor in New York turned out for this rare opportunity to appear on the newly 'liberated' screen. Jones himself was rejected as 'inexperienced'. The more things change, etc.

Ford, however, did change many of his old movie attitudes towards blacks, Indians and women through the Fifties and Sixties. Or perhaps he merely allowed the tide of history to sweep him along. He did not always seem comfortable on the new terrain. *The Horse Soldiers*, with liberal mouthpiece William Holden repeatedly sassing straight soldier John Wayne, seemed uncharacteristically rhetorical for a Ford film, and *Cheyenne Autumn*, with its impenetrably noble Indian protagonists, was an outright failure despite its good intentions. Thus, whereas the great moments in *The Horse Soldiers* – the children cadets on the march to drum and fife, the thin blue line of Union Cavalry strung across the horizon, the desperate charge of Confederate remnants at the railway station – are epical rather than rhetorical, the few redeeming moments in *Cheyenne Autumn* (mostly in the Wyatt Earp episode) are anecdotal rather than epical.

Ford's turnabout on the race issue between the Fifties and the Sixties can be traced in the shift of attitudes between the last farewell to Stepin' Fetchit as the lethargic darky menaced by a lynch mob in *The Sun Shines Bright*, and the legend-encrusted ballad ('Captain Buffalo') which welcomes Woody Strode in and as *Sergeant Rutledge*, a towering, virile, black, spit-and-polish cavalryman menaced by a court martial and hanging, largely because of racist taboos on the subject of his sexuality. Ford links the courtroom melodrama (by which Rutledge is vindicated) to the epic setting in Monument Valley (where Rutledge rides to glory and redemption) by means of a series of very carefully framed dolly shots inward, as if Ford were rewriting the Western genre to tell a story he was never able to tell before.

When Peter Bogdanovich asked Ford bluntly, 'Was the point of *Sergeant Rutledge* that the Negro's home was the Army?', Ford replied candidly, 'Yes, that's the point. The Negro soldier, the regular, is very proud. They had always been a cavalry outfit, but in this last war they were mechanized – they took their horses away, and they were broken-hearted. They were very proud of their outfit; they had great *esprit de corps*. I liked that picture. It was the first time we had ever shown the Negro as a hero.' Ford's response and the film itself raise more questions than they answer. From the point of view of the more militant blacks in the Sixties, *Sergeant Rutledge* was too little and too late. Negro *esprit de corps* in what was still basically a white man's army hardly seemed relevant to the anarchic thrust of black power. Indeed, *Sergeant Rutledge* seemed counter-revolutionary from a revisionist perspective in that blacks were being recruited on the screen by whites to continue the long genocidal campaign against the Indians. There has been a great deal of wishful thinking of the Third World variety both on and off the screen about the ultimate unity of all oppressed minorities. Hence, the ideal revisionist scenario pits the blacks and the Indians and even the nonconformists (vide *Little Big Man*) against the evil whites. Ford's alignment in *Sergeant Rutledge* is simpler to the point of fundamentalism: the Army (black and white) against the Indians; the innocent against the guilty.

Sergeant Rutledge must be innocent of the charge of raping and murdering a nubile white girl at an army post. He must be innocent even though he is found bending over her body by her horrified commandant father, even though he has to kill the misled father to save his own life, and even though he chooses to flee the post rather than try to explain his predicament to other white officers. Ford never shows the most crucial moments of racial misunderstanding on the screen; we learn of these moments only through courtroom testimony. But he very skilfully evokes these moments by staging a Gothic encounter (at night with the wind howling) between Sergeant Rutledge on the run and a white woman (Constance Towers) in

149

Sergeant Rutledge: Woody Strode, Constance Towers

distress. Out of this visual dialectic between the black and the blonde, Ford very honestly evokes all the fears inherent in the encounter before forging a chain of trust between the two racial elements in the communal equation.

But Rutledge must be innocent for the story to be told as Ford wants to tell it, and not only innocent, but disciplined and repressed as well. For all we see of military life in Sergeant Rutledge's cavalry command, the blacks might just as well be serving time in a monastery since there do not seem to be any female companions, black or white, with whom the troops can safely fraternize. Hence, Ford evokes the sexual tension between the races without making the slightest effort to explore the inner feelings of black sexuality. Instead, the abstractions of duty and justice are pursued to the truth-revealing dénouement in which Fred Libby's exposed murderer collapses to his knees with an abject contrition reminiscent of Ward Bond's guilt-ridden genuflection in *Young Mr Lincoln* two decades before. Rutledge is cleared and returned to his military monastery in time to provide a light-hearted ceremonial flourish for the perfunctorily resumed courtship between the film's romantic white leads, played with becoming Fordian modesty by Jeffrey Hunter and Constance Towers.

Still, though the implications of the story are disturbing and even distasteful from certain viewpoints, Ford's directorial rendering of the narrative is as masterful as ever. For some reason, Ford seems much closer to Strode's Rutledge than he is to the Indian protagonists in *Cheyenne Autumn*. Again, Ford is hardly unique in sentimentalizing a judicial issue by insisting on the absolute innocence of the accused. Such hitherto admired anti-lynch movies as Fritz Lang's *Fury* and William Wellman's *The Ox-Bow Incident* were also flawed by their facile advocacy of due process for the innocent rather than for the guilty. Hence *Sergeant Rutledge* has more to commend it than ideological fashions of the Sixties seemed to dictate. Though it does not attain the highest level of Ford's art, it remains a fascinating achievement in distanced storytelling.

Even more underrated has been *Two Rode Together*, a dark, savage movie which even Ford seems to have dismissed as a casual favour to Columbia studio mogul Harry Cohn. Both François Truffaut (in *Jules and Jim*) and Peter Bogdanovich (in *The Last Picture Show*) have frankly imitated Ford's single-take riverside conversation between James Stewart's lanky opportunist and Richard Widmark's uniformed idealist, one of the screen's most memorable images of amiable communion between friends, more beautiful by far through Ford's intuitive decision to stop at the bend of the river to take stock than through both Truffaut's and Bogdanovich's more cerebral decisions to apply a classical figure of style to their own scenarios. One might say indeed that Truffaut's borrowing from Ford is in this instance too lyrically *nouvelle*, and Bogdanovich's too mechanically *nouveau*.

At the time I first considered *Two Rode Together* in print (in *NY Film Bulletin* for its 1961 year's-end issue) I was caught up in the polemical and political fever of the period, but I still stand by my intense feelings of discovery and revaluation:

John Ford, America's Renoir, has been directing movies for forty-four years. It is no longer advisable to pick off his films one by one even when they open on the circuits. Of course, anything is possible for reviewers who still subscribe to the 'happy accident' theory of film-making. In *Two Rode Together*, Ford returns to the Comanche-infested Southwest of *The Searchers* where the director has thrown in his lot with the scattered remnants of the Confederacy and the Spanish-American Catholic aristocracy. The classical Ford images of Indian war parties, frontier dances and cavalry formations are subtly debased and dusted over in the dim twilight of the Western epic. With Yankee hypocrisy and hysteria engulfing the frontier,

151

Two Rode Together: Woody Strode, James Stewart

Ford's cynical hero rides off on a false crusade to repatriate white captives. The Indian camp, divided into rival trader and warrior factions, is sketched with appropriate Moscow–Peking shadings, and the emotional frenzy of foolish crusaders recalls through parallel perception the fruitless wailing outside the Brandenburg Gate and along the China Coast. Ford disposes of the settlers and their volatile convictions with a whirlwind lynching composed of a series of fluently edited sweeping movements and a 'rosebud' plot climax, which reminds us that Orson Welles studied *Stagecoach* intensively before making *Citizen Kane*. Who else but Ford would cast Woody Strode, a Negro actor, as the virile Comanche who challenges James Stewart for possession of a Mexican captive squaw? (Ford can be cited as a past offender in the Stepin' Fetchit school of darky caricatures, but when he finally employed the Negro as a protagonist in *Sergeant Rutledge*, he cut to the raw nerve of the racial 'problem' by recreating the sexual nightmare in which the white man transfers his guilt and insecurity to the Negro.) In *Two Rode Together*, the image of Stewart's taking root in a spread-legged arch after shooting Strode is a monument of the masculine cinema in a neurotic age.

If my critical tone in 1962 sounds unduly strident in the 1970s, I can say in its defence only that there seemed to be a real danger at the time that John Ford would become a non-person in supposedly serious film histories. Even in Paris, where I had spent most of 1961, the critical climate was still chilly to Ford's new ventures, and for all I knew at the time, Ford's professional survival might have been in jeopardy.

Even by the summer of 1963 I still felt the need to legitimize Ford's career for a readership which seemed hostile to any intimation of his continued existence. But I began to wonder also if my critical efforts (now in *The Village Voice*) were becoming counterproductive. Hence a certain diffidence in my declarations, as if I were trying to enhance Ford at my own expense, perhaps even to trick the reader into discovering Ford without seeming to have been driven in that direction. Only very much later did it turn out that a highly regarded new Seventies director like Martin Scorsese had been so inspired by *Donovan's Reef* at the time that he was to insert Wayne–Marvin brawl footage from the film a decade later in his own first big hit, *Mean Streets*. But in 1963, I was still a lonely voice as I sang the praises of what turned out to be Ford's most escapist film ever:

Donovan's Reef is John Ford's *Picnic on the Grass* just as *Picnic on the Grass* is Jean Renoir's *The Tempest*, the ultimate distillation of an old artist's serenity and wisdom. The delicate brush strokes of characterization have now been blurred over by the buoyant mists of a personal vision, and, consequently, a psychological analysis of the characters in *Donovan's Reef* would have as much point as a case history of Caliban.

There are directors who discover the world and directors who invent it. Ford and most of his Hollywood colleagues belong in the second category, where the cinema has always been more a dream than a document. In the realm of escapism, however, Ford has gone Walker Percy's *The Moviegoer* one better. Whereas Percy's protagonist merely discovers that the movies certify reality and that a place is not a place until it has been reproduced on the screen, Ford manipulates reality to certify the movies.

As if to commemorate all the Hawaiian and Tahitian sarong epics contrived on the Hollywood back lots over the years, Ford sailed off to Kauai, Hawaii, simply to conjure up the natural background for the Hollywood myth, reincarnated in the gallant gaucherie of Dorothy Lamour on the imaginary atoll of Haleakoloha, a realm governed by the suave French (Cesar Romero), operated by brawling Americans (John Wayne, Lee Marvin, Jack Warden), intrigue-ridden by the wily Chinese (Jon Fong), invaded by the truculent Australians (Dick Foran and one chorus of 'Waltzing Matilda'), merchandised by the ingenious Japanese, and restrained by the Catholic Church (Marcel Dalio). Add a Boston millionairess spinster (Elizabeth Allen) coming to check up on her errant father (Warden) and staying to perform a modified strip-tease for her elective affinity (Wayne),

Donovan's Reef: the Wayne–Marvin brawl

stir nicely with an ineffable Christmas Pageant in Ford's hierarchical Paradise, and serve up as one apparently effortless hot-weather entertainment.

I must confess the temptation to let the matter rest right there by obeying A. E. Housman's astute warning that perfect understanding will sometimes almost extinguish pleasure. Why should I argue that Ford is a director for all seasons when even the dreariest of the realistic critics acknowledge Ford's expertise with froth? This is the problem of that multivalent art which can (and should) be understood on many levels. There is an awesome consistency to Ford's vision of life. Over and over again, he has demonstrated that the free life is a function of order and tradition, and that we must all belong somewhere before we can allow our impulses to govern our actions. The blissful world of *Donovan's Reef* is not the anarchic world of the Noble Savage. The lines of responsibility cut deep into the sun-baked flesh. Whether it is Church, State, Community, Army or simply remembered service, the characters of John Ford acknowledge certain limits to their power and discretion in the form of a superior authority. There is always someone somewhere who can step into the midst of the wildest brawl and make the combatants snap to attention not through mere physical force, nor even personal authority, but through a freely granted power to remind muscular brutes of their chivalric calling. Yet by any interpretation, *Donovan's Reef* is a beautiful example of cinematic art, and the atavistic desire to let the movie sweep over the spectator without disruptive analysis is at least understandable.

Mogambo is almost, but not quite, in the same category of edifyingly escapist entertainment as *Donovan's Reef*. Let us say simply that *Mogambo* is a less personal project, the work more of a *metteur en scène*, however accomplished, than of an *auteur*. *Mogambo* was remade not only from another director's movie (Victor Fleming's *Red Dust*); it was remade also from one of the most charismatic big-star hits of the Thirties. One would never have thought that a Fifties cast could have regenerated the erotic electricity of Clark Gable, Jean Harlow and Mary Astor back in the Thirties. If anything, an older Clark Gable, a sultry-cynical Ava Gardner, and a squeamish-sensual Grace Kelly even topped the original trio. Furthermore, the remake executes the original's slick dramatic effects with equal élan. And in the *mise en scène* round the edges of this Great White Hunter melodrama, there is obviously no comparison between Ford and Fleming.

Metro was a good studio for Ford in the Fifties in that *Mogambo* and the sublime *The Wings of Eagles* were among his handsomest and most visually resourceful productions away from Monument Valley. What is strange is that despite the virtual flawlessness of *Mogambo* as escapist big-star entertainment, it seems to have left no mark in film history even among popcorn-oriented film critics. And where are the pop odes to Ava Gardner to compare with those lavished so profusely and so ritualistically on the late Marilyn Monroe? Without taking anything away from the ill-fated Monroe, it is impossible to dredge up out of her spotty filmography as many memorable incarnations of intelligent, grown-up sensuality as Ava Gardner projected in Robert Siodmak's *The Killers*, Albert Lewin's *Pandora and the Flying Dutchman*, Joseph L. Mankiewicz's *The Barefoot Contessa*, George Cukor's *Bhowani Junction*, and, most appealingly of all, Ford's *Mogambo*, in which she brings the old lion out of Gable to an extent that not even Harlow, much less Monroe, ever approached. *Mogambo* ranks alongside *The Whole Town's Talking* as one of Ford's most enjoyable entertainments for people who never heard of John Ford and who could not care less about his personal themes and obsessions.

What then are Ford's most profound achievements in his late period as film poet without portfolio? I would cite six films (in chronological order): *She Wore a Yellow Ribbon, Wagonmaster, Rio Grande, The Searchers, Wings of Eagles* and *The Man Who Shot Liberty*

Valance. I can make stronger and more thoughtfully reasoned cases for some of these films than for others. I am most uncertain about *She Wore a Yellow Ribbon* and *Rio Grande*, not only because they seem incomplete without *Fort Apache*, but also because there seems to be something more tentative than intuitive in Ford's ideas about them, as if he were drifting in an obscure reverie for which he had not found an articulated form. Ford seems to have lost his taste for violence and warfare as he got older, and consequently both *She Wore a Yellow Ribbon* and *Rio Grande* seem to abound in lyrical and metaphysical circumlocutions designed to avoid conflict and confrontation as long as possible.

In a sense, *She Wore a Yellow Ribbon* and *Rio Grande* are refinements of *Fort Apache* rather than sequels to it. Even when considered as Ford's 'unofficial' Cavalry trilogy, the three films are curiously anomalous. *Fort Apache* and *Rio Grande* are in black and white and *She Wore a Yellow Ribbon* is in colour, indeed a colour so striking that the film has been singled out by film historians for that fact alone. Frank S. Nugent worked on the screenplays of *Fort Apache* and *She Wore a Yellow Ribbon*, but not on *Rio Grande*. Yet John Wayne plays the same character years apart in *Fort Apache* (Capt. Kirby York) and *Rio Grande* (Lt.-Col. Kirby York), but an entirely different character (Capt. Nathan Brittles) in *She Wore a Yellow Ribbon*. Wayne himself plays youngish in *Fort Apache*, oldish in *She Wore a Yellow Ribbon*, and indeterminately middle-aged in *Rio Grande*. Although the three films were released within two and a half years, Ford did three other pictures in the same period, the most important of which was *Wagonmaster*, a film with a rollicking ballad gusto which seems to have carried over into *Rio Grande*, and which gives *Rio Grande* a somewhat looser form and more intimate focus than either *Fort Apache* or *She Wore a Yellow Ribbon*. One might say that in *Fort Apache* the emphasis is epic and the protagonist is the Cavalry, whereas in *She Wore a Yellow Ribbon* the emphasis is psychological and the protagonists are individual Cavalry officers and their loved ones. Still, most Ford scholars have tended to downgrade *Fort Apache* in comparison with *She Wore a Yellow Ribbon* and even *Rio Grande*. Certainly, Ford pays a price for his sentimental gesture to Shirley Temple in *Fort Apache*; and Joanne Dru in *She Wore a Yellow Ribbon* and Maureen O'Hara in *Rio Grande* are undeniably a vast improvement.

Rio Grande

None the less, *Fort Apache* is graced with a narrative more coherent and more structured than that of either *She Wore a Yellow Ribbon* or *Rio Grande*. The dramatic issues in *Fort Apache* are clearly drawn and violently resolved amid a cloud of dust and a classical Apache ambush. By contrast, *She Wore a Yellow Ribbon* and *Rio Grande* tend to drift from incident to incident into picturesque reveries of retreat and resignation. Thus, whereas John Wayne's performance in *Fort Apache* gets its cutting edge from scraping against the rock-like integrity of Henry Fonda's performance (itself reminiscent of Robert Montgomery's solid ballast for Wayne's bobbing and weaving in *They Were Expendable*), Wayne's portrayals in *She Wore a Yellow Ribbon* and *Rio Grande* float freely in a sea of communal and conjugal feeling. In *She Wore a Yellow Ribbon* Wayne's mission is that of the ageing peace-maker seeking to avert the very kind of Apache–Army battle which Ford staged so rousingly in *Fort Apache*. In a sense, the pacifist orientation of *She Wore a Yellow Ribbon* takes Ford away from the dynamics of his

157

She Wore a Yellow Ribbon: 'picturesque reveries of retreat'

own genre, since the movie is ultimately about a battle that was never fought.

And although there is more of a battle in *Rio Grande*, there too the focus shifts from the frontier wars to the family reunion of a cavalry officer with his estranged wife and son. The last shot of the film unites husband and wife – Wayne on a litter, and a very concerned Maureen O'Hara walking alongside – more than it marks the end of a successful campaign. The distance at which Ford's camera contemplates the spectacle helps to establish this indelible image of the wife as a ministering angel, but there is more to the relationship than the focal length of a lens, however intuitively appropriate the choice of distance may seem in retrospect.

It is perhaps symptomatic of Ford's Catholicism that his characters should suffer through long separations without starting their lives anew. Thus while the Protestant protagonists of Howard Hawks seem more at home in the wilderness because of their inexhaustible capacity for reinventing the terms of their existence, John Ford's characters remain confined within old memories and old allegiances. If Hawksian cinema is the cinema of regeneration, Fordian cinema is the cinema of reminiscence. The Hawksian hero excels; the Fordian hero endures. Whereas the Hawksian hero tends to forget his past, the Fordian hero tends to treasure his memories. In this context one might compare the funeral services in *Red River* with those in *She Wore a Yellow Ribbon*. The Hawks service is almost laughingly laconic, as if life were too precious to be squandered on the rites of death. In a Ford film the mourning hero talks more eloquently to the dead than to the living. Indeed, the bonds of emotional attachment are more securely fastened beyond the grave than ever they were on earth.

It is ultimately a mistake to think of Ford's films as typical expressions of any genre, least of all the Western. Talking about his reasons for undertaking *Cheyenne Autumn*, Ford told Peter Bogdanovich: 'I had wanted to make it for a long time. I've killed more Indians than Custer, Beecher and Chivington put together, and people in Europe always want to know about the Indians.' There are two striking incongruities in Ford's statement: first, his assumption of more genocidal guilt than his own films have actually earned in the way of a hard and fast body count, and, second, his disconcertingly sophisticated awareness that his reputation was more secure abroad than at home, and that, indeed, towards the end of his career he remained commercially and critically viable only because of the European market.

The great majority of redskins who bit the dust on the screen owe their downfall less to Ford than to a horde of hack directors, second-unit specialists and stunt-men. Ford may have supplied many of the most graphic images of the Indian Wars, but he never dwelt inordinately on the slaughter. Nor are Westerns most appealing to their adult admirers when the screen is cluttered with rampaging Indians. Quite the contrary: the Western genre expresses itself more eloquently through space than through mass, and so through a narrative of personal destiny rather than of collective consciousness-raising. But the screen's satirists of Westerns (*vide* the endless Indian charge on Jack Lemmon's television set in Billy Wilder's *The Apartment*) prefer to dismiss all Westerns as mindless mob spectacles. Unfortunately, the satirists have succeeded too well in discouraging big city attendance at even the most entertaining Westerns. To the immediate point, Ford revivals and retrospectives have usually done badly even by museum standards.

To whom then was Ford really addressing *Cheyenne Autumn*? Not to the Indians certainly. They were beyond caring. Not to the hard-core Western audiences here and abroad. They were hardly to be wooed with a revisionist romance. Could it be instead that Ford made *Cheyenne Autumn* as one last hopeful gesture to the New York

Cheyenne Autumn: 'the dignity of the Other'

critical establishment? Towards the end of that very year (1965), Bosley Crowther of the *New York Times* rose at the annual meeting of the New York Film Critics Circle to propose a special award to Ford for a lifetime of achievement, but the motion was tabled by a majority of the members.

The point to be made here is that the John Ford of *She Wore a Yellow Ribbon* and *Wagonmaster* had no need to do penance in the form of *Cheyenne Autumn*, at least not for himself and for his own films. It is not that he had ever succeeded, even in *Cheyenne Autumn*, in seeing the West through the eyes of the Indian. What American film-maker actually has? But even in Ford's most morbidly obsessive ruminations on the Redman (notably in *The Searchers* and *Two Rode Together*), he had always scrupulously respected the dignity and honour of the Other in the remorselessly racist dialectic of the genre. Besides, Ford never exploited the Western to exult over the westward thrust of Manifest Destiny. His protagonists are not conquerors in search of new riches, but rather pilgrims in search of the Holy Grail of *Grandeur et Servitude*. It is therefore fittingly Fordian that the John Wayne character in *The Man Who Shot Liberty Valance* jokingly addresses the James Stewart character as 'Pilgrim', and that the sobriquet not only sticks but resonates with religious fervour.

There is a change in Ford's films over the years, but never anything that might be termed revisionism. Ford never lost his faith in the benign drift of American history. Even in his most left-leaning period represented by *The Grapes of Wrath* and *How Green Was My Valley*, Ford intuitively redirected the pessimistic class conflicts in the Steinbeck and Llewellyn novels into relatively optimistic family chronicles. At this point in his career Ford was at once nostalgic and progressive. His prize-winning works exuded faith in the future, a faith partly derived from the evangelical naïveté of the period, and partly from his own artistic pre-eminence as a film-maker. But as he got older, the collective dreams of the Forties degenerated into the cacophonous divisiveness of the Fifties and Sixties. As Ford willed himself more and more into the past, his conservatism came to the fore. His imagery became ever more archetypal, his gestures ever more sacramental, and his characters ever more resigned to their fates.

Even so, Ford never inflated his feelings with rhetorical bombast. Unfortunately, the tactful nuances of Ford's style have often been overlooked by his detractors because of their tendency to treat every Western alike, if not indeed interchangeably. The critical impasse over John Wayne's iconography is instructive in this regard. Through the Sixties and Seventies John Wayne mockingly complained at public gatherings that in the old Westerns the antagonists shot each other to death whereas in the new, adult Westerns they preferred to talk each other to death. Curiously, the strong, silent persona which Wayne sought to project with this joke was verbosely betrayed by his own self-directed vehicles, *The Alamo* and *The Green Berets*. Left to his own devices (and direction), Wayne transformed these patriotic spectacles into tedious talkfests. By contrast, Ford had become a legend in his own time for paring down the dialogue passages from his films. Hence, the laconic Wayne warhorse was largely the product of the wordless lacunae in Ford's staging of scenes. Similarly, Wayne's machismo mannerisms in loutish lapses like John Farrow's *Hondo* (with its dreadful denigration of Geraldine Page) and Andrew McLaglen's *McClintock* (with its public spanking of Maureen O'Hara) are too often carelessly charged against Ford's more balanced account with Wayne. As it happens, *Hondo* and *McClintock* are light years away aesthetically from *She Wore a Yellow Ribbon, Rio Grande, The Searchers, Wings of Eagles* and

'Who seemed to have been born on a horse': Ben Johnson in *Wagonmaster*

The Man Who Shot Liberty Valance. But it is difficult to impart this elementary insight to people who persist in seeing the fortuitously intersecting careers of Ford and Wayne through the wrong end of the telescope.

Ford was fortunate also in discovering Ben Johnson when he did, first to buttress Wayne in *She Wore a Yellow Ribbon* and *Rio Grande,* and then to burst through on his own in *Wagonmaster,* the movie that should have made him an action star in the Fifties, but somehow did not. At the time the critical community seemed attuned more to allegory than to action, and more to realism than to romance. It seemed that only Ford could properly appreciate a natural performer like Johnson, who seemed to have been born on a horse. Hence, after *Wagonmaster,* Johnson drifted into villainous roles for other directors, most notably as the bloodied barroom Goliath to Alan Ladd's deadpan David in George Stevens' *Shane.* In one very forgettable Western Johnson played the villain to the hero of Ben Cooper, a doe-eyed male ingénu who was clearly more 'sensitive' than Johnson. Even Johnson's physical stature was a handicap in a decade dominated by such diminutive Method analysands as Marlon Brando, Montgomery Clift and James Dean. Two decades after the false dawn of *Wagonmaster*, Ben Johnson was resurrected by Peter Bogdanovich in *The Last Picture Show*, for which he won an Oscar, after which he was used prominently by such neo-action directors as Sam Peckinpah (*The Getaway*), James Frawley (*Kid Blue*), John Milius (*Dillinger*) and Steven Spielberg (*The Sugarland Express*).

In the *New York Film Bulletin* of 27 March, 1961, I took a very polemical position vis à vis a revival of *Wagonmaster*:

It can be argued that *Wagonmaster* is John Ford's greatest film. If I choose not to argue the point at this time, it is because there are too many other candidates to consider, and these do not include *The Informer* and *The Grapes of Wrath*. *Wagonmaster* has only fragments of a plot. A wagon train of Mormon settlers are led to a promised land by a young horse trader. They encounter deserts and mountains, Indians and outlaws, and even encompass a traveling medicine show that provides a strange romance for the horse trader turned wagonmaster. Well served by an unmannered cast led by Ben Johnson, Joanne Dru and Ward Bond, Ford does not waste any time over the subtleties of characterization and twists of plot. He strokes boldly across the canvas of the American past as he concentrates on the evocative images of a folk tradition that no other American director has ever been able to render. It is a tradition of free adventure and compelling adaptability. There are no moral shadings. His villains are evil incarnate – whining, wheedling and uselessly destructive. The hero destroys them in the end as he would destroy a snake, and the sophisticated medicine-show girl smiles inscrutably as she realizes without an exchange of words that she is destined for this virile 'rube'. There are the Mormon square dances and the unforgettable circular stomp of friendly Indians. Above all, there are the wagons themselves, those symbolic vehicles that remind us that John Ford's *Stagecoach* initiated the modern American cinema.

If I choose to preserve the hyperbole and oversimplification of the preceding passage, it is because the critical climate in which my anger was articulated has not changed appreciably since the early Sixties. Films like *Wagonmaster* and *Wings of Eagles* should have been long since enshrined as Fifties' classics; they remain instead cultist causes. The films themselves have been written off by much of

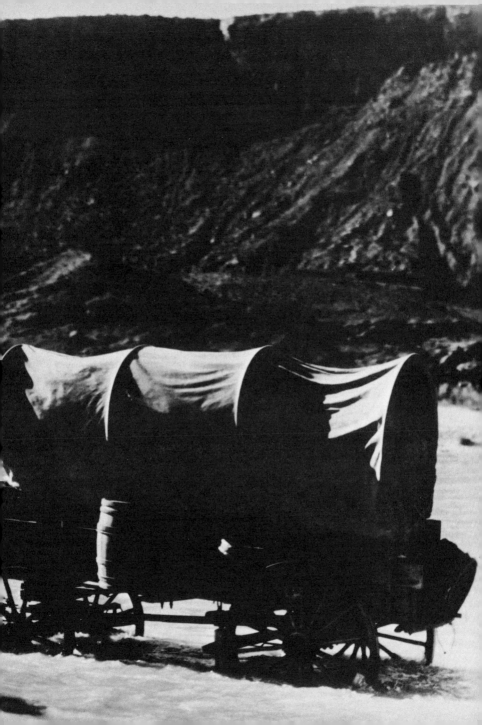

the American critical establishment for celebrating values that seem not only obsolete but downright reactionary.

Ford did not contribute to the Fifties' chic of *Wagonmaster* by saturating its soundtrack (and that of *Rio Grande* as well) with the buckskin ballads of the Sons of the Pioneers. Yet *Wagonmaster* is one of the few Ford Westerns which is forward-looking rather than backward-looking. It is as if Ford had found in the Mormons a truly moral pioneer stock, a people obsessed less with conquering the continent than with sharing it with all and sundry. For once, the plot has been ingeniously contrived to reinforce the theme of accommodation. Hence, Ben Johnson's force-renouncing hero loses face for the longest time in order to save lives. Badgered both by Ward Bond's bewildered elder and Harry Carey Jr's gun-cocking youth in search of his manhood, the hero follows his own prudent course, and finally assumes the classical role of the avenger only when the villains jeopardize the survival of the entire group. The rubber band of restraint is stretched just about as far as it can go this side of ignoble masochism before it snaps with explosive fury and deadly finality. The actual violence takes up a tiny portion of screen time, less really than is consumed by a single chorus from the Sons of the Pioneers. Thus, *Wagonmaster* is ultimately a film about life rather than death, about survival rather than extinction. It is perhaps too happy a work ever to be truly fashionable.

Whereas *Wagonmaster* provides at least genre covering against the foul winds of fashion, *Wings of Eagles* stands naked before its enemies in the modern world. Ford himself did not like the studio's grandiose title for what had been originally intended as a modest biography of Frank W. 'Spig' Wead, Ford's scenarist for *Air Mail* and *They Were Expendable*, who also wrote *Ceiling Zero* (Howard Hawks), *Dirigible* (Frank Capra) and *Hell Divers* (George Hill). There is an interesting clip from *Hell Divers* in *Wings of Eagles*, interesting not so much because of the clip itself with its roisterous brawl between Wallace Beery and Clark Gable back in 1932, but because of the layers of Pirandellianism in Ward Bond's portrayal of a Hollywood director named John Dodge, a dodge indeed for an old University of Maine football player named 'Bull' Feeney.

In purely biographical terms, John Dodge should stand for the late George Hill, the director of *Hell Divers*, but Bond and Ford chose

The Wings of Eagles: the grounding of a flier (John Wayne)

instead to leave a legacy of Bond's mischievous imitation of Ford. There are many memorabilia – Ford's 'In Conference' couch for snoozing, his hollow cane for boozing, his Oscars and trophies, his pipe and his hat. All in all, Bond's Ford reflects Ford's own somewhat satirical ambivalence towards the essentially passive, voyeuristic, exploitational role of the Hollywood director. There is no malice in the performance, but no self-glorification either. There was always a real world out beyond the set to which Ford owed his primary emotional allegiance. And the story of Spig Wead is the story of a traveller from that real world of naval aviation to its lurid counterfeit in show business. With John Wayne's Wead especially we do not so much glory in the emergence of an artist from a crippling fall as we mourn the grounding of a flier whose wings have been clipped by adversity. *Wings of Eagles* thus becomes a poetic parable of Ford's lifelong yearning for a life of action. The opening sequences are played with disconcerting broadness, and with too precise a slapstick rhythm to be effectively funny. Dan Dailey is particularly indefatigable as the comedy relief and lower-grade life force, and he is but one of many onlookers to the sombre saga of Spig Wead.

In its way *Wings of Eagles* is as relentless a record of pain and loss as *Citizen Kane*. At the start Wead loses his infant son to death, then his wife to duty. Ultimately, he loses even the physical capacity to serve his country, and he is slung over the side from his beloved carrier to a smaller ship and from there to an enforced retirement on land, and, not much later presumably, beneath the earth. Ford sees to it that Wead's whole life passes before him and us, a life that he never had a chance to live fully. But if *Wings of Eagles* expresses a feeling of loss, it is too dutiful a document to express a feeling of waste. The truly fashionable film of 1957 was David Lean's *The Bridge on the River Kwai*, with its massive dosage of irony and cynicism regarding World War II. Ford was having none of this revisionist absurdism. He still believed in the righteousness of the cause in which he had served. But if his devotion to duty and his unregenerate flagwaving were all that were to be said about Ford's art, he would be a minor figure indeed in film history. Of course, we can talk about his impeccable instinct for cutting and continuity, his long shot integrity in filming epic spectacles, the integrity that so impressed and influenced Welles, Kazan and Bogdanovich. But after a point we would be ducking the main issues of his art. Of Ford's talent there has never been any serious doubt, but on the exact size of his moral vision and artistic achievement there still remains considerable controversy. I happen to think that *Wings of Eagles* is infinitely superior to *The Bridge on the River Kwai*, and I can defend my preference shot by shot, and in terms of the organic unity and consistency of a work of art. I would be deceiving myself, however, if I did not acknowledge also that I was more receptive to what the Ford film was saying and showing than to what the Lean film was saying and showing. From these two works, at least, the life of duty seems emotionally more compelling than the life of doubt.

In addition, *The Wings of Eagles* is the final flowering of Ford's romantic tribute to his most fiercely attracted couple, John Wayne and Maureen O'Hara, hitherto consecrated in *The Quiet Man* and *Rio Grande*, but here taken through decades of longing and frustration. Ford does not subordinate the marital side of Wead to his military side, but stresses their ultimate incompatibility. Indeed, Ford endows the marriage with great beauty and sensuality, and he

The Wings of Eagles: Wayne and O'Hara

tries to come to terms even with the very strange form of neurotic modern woman expressed by Maureen O'Hara in a veritable orgy of chain-smoking and record smashing. But Miss O'Hara is most arresting when Ford is looking at her mutely through his own and Wayne's humbled eyes. Ford's gaze is often strikingly oblique (*vide* the upside-down mirror shot of O'Hara downstairs and outside from Wayne's hospital bed), as if the sacred beauty of the subject were too dazzling to be stared at directly. Ford's love and awe for women is never in question, and he fully accepts and even admires their intelligence. Where he is deficient in the depiction of women is in treating them so solemnly that he deprives them of humour and irony. Like so many devoted part-time admirers of women, Ford cannot imagine their occasional indifference to their supposedly sacred relationships. This deficiency is less damaging to *Wings of Eagles*, with its built-in emphasis on Wead, than to a woman-written project like *Seven Women*, in which its most knowingly humorous dimension is sacrificed to Ford's unyielding reverence for the fair sex. But if Ford

169

had had more humour, would he have had less feeling? This is one of the insoluble mysteries of all art and all artists. In Proust's parlance, how often when we say in spite of do we really mean because?

The Searchers was greeted with mild bafflement by American reviewers in 1956. Adapted from the Alan LeMay novel by Frank S. Nugent, the film reflects Ford's final abandonment of the dramatic ironies of Nichols for the epic directness of Nugent. The Fifties were characterized by the breakdown of traditional notions of the well-made film through an eruption of stylistic ambition. 1956 was the year also of such official 'big' pictures as George Stevens' *Giant*, John Huston's *Moby Dick*, William Wyler's *Friendly Persuasion* and Laurence Olivier's *Richard III*. Even for the conventional reviewers of the period, however, there was something flawed, unwieldy and heavy about these preconceived classics. And so the critical consensus settled upon *Around the World in 80 Days*, a producer's package of highly publicized cameo vaudeville bits glossed over with the superciliousness of an alleged S. J. Perelman script that later became the cause of litigation with two other screenwriters. Between the establishment classics and Michael Todd's camp curiosity there was a group of obsessively picaresque movies which were appreciated only in the pages of adventurous French film magazines. Among these were *The Searchers*, Alfred Hitchcock's expansive remake of *The Man Who Knew Too Much*, George Cukor's deliriously dream-like *Bhowani Junction*, Budd Boetticher's monumentally vengeful *Seven Men From Now*, and even Cecil B. DeMille's awesomely archaic *The Ten Commandments*. And the best of these is still *The Searchers*, which manages to sum up stylistically all the best of what Ford had been with all the best of what he was to be.

The innate pictorialism of Ford's style, evident as early as 1917 in *Straight Shooting*, finds in *The Searchers* a majestically familial context in the very first shot of a door opening on to the screen and the world and the past, extending outwards to a solitary figure inching his way forward to the enclosure, the sanctuary, the long-lost home, the full measure of his aching aspirations. None the less Ford's pictorialism is just angular enough and windswept enough to avoid the too contrivedly concentric compositions of George Stevens' *Shane*, in which a deer turns its head at that precise moment when its antlers will frame the mysterious horseman (Alan Ladd) in the

170

The Searchers

distance. But then *Shane* is storybook (and storyboard) myth *par excellence*, whereas *The Searchers* is lived-in epic with the kind of landscaped pastness across which the characters hang up their laundry and other hang-ups.

The Searchers is concerned as much with a peculiarly American wanderlust as with anything else. Some of the characters start out mad, some achieve madness, and some have madness thrust upon them. Ford's world accommodates madness as it accommodates everything else, and with madness there is wisdom and robust humour, as with Mose Harper (Hank Worden), a certified lunatic who asks only to while away his last days in a rocking chair by a fireplace, and who gains his rocking chair for services rendered (to Ford as well as to John Wayne's Ethan Edwards).

Very early in *The Searchers* there is an intricate sequence (which I described in some detail in *The American Cinema*) involving a brash frontier character played by Ward Bond. This bumptious Bond character is drinking a cup of coffee in a standing-up position before going out to hunt some Comanches. He glances towards one of the bedrooms, and notices the woman of the house tenderly caressing the Army uniform of her husband's brother. Ford cuts back to a full-faced shot of Bond drinking his coffee, his eyes tactfully averted from the intimate scene he had just witnessed. Nothing on earth would ever force this man to reveal what he had seen. There is a deep, subtle chivalry at work here, and in most of Ford's films, but it is never obtrusive enough to interfere with the flow of the narrative. The delicacy of emotion expressed here in three quick shots, perfectly cut, framed and distanced, would completely escape the dulled perception of our more cosmopolitan critics even if they deigned to consider a despised genre like the Western. The economy of expression that Ford had achieved in fifty years of film-making constituted the beauty of his style. If it had taken him any longer than three shots and a few seconds to establish this insight into the Bond character, the point would not be worth making. Ford would have been false to the manners of a time and a place bounded by the rigorous necessity of survival.

Yet when Peter Bogdanovich asked Ford: 'Was the scene, towards the beginning, during which Wayne's sister-in-law gets his coat for him, meant to convey silently a past love between them?' Ford answered somewhat gruffly: 'Well, I thought it was pretty obvious — that his brother's wife was in love with Wayne; you couldn't hit it on the nose, but I think it's very plain to anyone with any intelligence. You could tell from the way she picked up his.cape and I think you could tell from Ward Bond's expression and from his exit — as though he hadn't noticed anything.' The scene may be 'obvious' now that we have been alerted to the larger implications of *The Searchers*, but in its own time, like Poe's purloined letter, it was overlooked because of rather than in spite of its very obviousness. The intended emotion seems early and misplaced. We have just met the characters involved, and we have no inkling that this will be absolutely the last opportunity for a faded frontierswoman (Dorothy Jordan) to express, however covertly, the forbidden feelings of a lost love. We are dealing here with lives that are almost over, and the dreadful constriction of time running out is felt in the pinched awkwardness and cramped closeness of the domestic scenes involving a group of people variously doomed to slaughter, captivity, revenge, before the final moments, two hours (screen time) and several years (narrative time) later, when a man picks up a girl in his arms and is miraculously delivered of all the racist, revenge-seeking furies that have seared his soul.

Jean-Luc Godard once observed that as much as he despised the reactionary politics of John Wayne he could never help but be moved by the emotional sweep of the awesomely avuncular gesture with which Wayne gathers up Natalie Wood, after having given every indication that he wished to kill her for defiling his sacred memories of a little girl accepting his medal as a token of his chivalric devotion to her mother. Deep down we do not really expect him to kill her, any more than we expect Wayne to kill Montgomery Clift in Hawks' *Red River*. Still, the *dénouement* of *The Searchers* is infinitely more moving and artistically satisfying than that of *Red River*, even discounting the intrusion of Joanne Dru's *deus ex machina* in the latter film. Part of the disparity of emotional effect can be attributed to the philosophical distinction between two visual styles – Hawks the eye-level vision of man as the measure of all things, Ford the double vision (through classical editing) of an event in all its vital immediacy, and yet also in its ultimate memory image on the horizon of history.

Hence, the dramatic struggle of *The Searchers* is not waged between a protagonist and an antagonist, or indeed between two protagonists as antagonists, but rather within the protagonist himself. Jeffrey Hunter's surrogate son figure in *The Searchers* is the witness to Wayne's struggle with himself rather than a force in resolving it. The mystery of the film is what has actually happened to Wayne in that fearsome moment when he discovers the mutilated bodies of his brother, his beloved sister-in-law, his nephew, and later his niece. Surly, cryptic, almost menacing even before the slaughter, he is invested afterwards with obsession and implacability. We in the audience never see the bodies or the actual slaughter, only the smoke passing across Wayne's contorted countenance at the moment of discovery, a cosmic composition of man ravaged by revenge-seeking emotions in the aftermath of an atrocity; but that cosmic composition, reprinted so often in specialized film magazines, never breaks the flow of action, but instead accelerates the development of characters, and cracks open, as violence traditionally does in drama, all their massively encrusted psychological secrets.

The Searchers is rich in the colours and textures of the seasons and the elements, from the whiteness of winter snows to the brownness of summer sands. When Wayne pledges his implacable presence at the last hiding place of his niece's Comanche captors ('as sure as the earth turns'), the film switches seasons with a swiftness that augments the planetary majesty of Wayne's turn of phrase. And with the change of seasons come changes in the searchers, changes of costume, mood and even silhouette. The startling sight of Wayne in a sombrero is the final confirmation of seasonal and regional adjustments in the conventions of a genre. Indeed, few Westerns even in the so-called revisionist mould are so resolutely untraditional in their trappings. Ward Bond's Texas Ranger wears a stovepipe derby, and the rifles are sensibly if tackily sheathed to keep out the dust. The only *bona fide* gunfight between good guys and bad guys ends with the bad guys shot in the back and robbed besides. Ford and Wayne tried as long before as *Stagecoach* (1939) to introduce suspenders to the standard Western costume, and they failed ignominiously.

Ford's humour is, as always, more ritualistic than mirthful. I must confess that I found it eminently resistible back in the Forties and Fifties when, like most of the critical establishment, I was unable to discern and describe the emotional connections in the new direction that Ford had taken. It was not until the Sixties that the rugged frontier slapstick of *The Searchers* could be appreciated as a necessary relaxation of the frightful tensions within the characters. The community involvement to which Ford's slapstick tends (with the help of reaction shots, that banal bugaboo of modern *cinéastes*) reduces some of the overwhelming solitude felt by the protagonist, and thus intensifies our own awareness of feelings that are all the more vivid for being momentarily relieved. It is much easier to see now than it was in 1956 that if Ford had been more solemn, *The Searchers* would have been less sublime.

It is our misfortune as film critics that we must discuss a film one-thing-at-a-time when on a screen so many things are happening and reverberating at the same time. How to evoke, for example, the

The Searchers: the end of the search (Natalie Wood, John Wayne, Jeffrey Hunter)

geometric convergence of three columns of horsemen, two Indian, one Texan, against the evocative magnificence of Monument Valley, Ford's own slice of stylized nature. All we can suggest is that Ford began film-making as a painter, and added poetry and music as he went along. In these terms, *The Searchers* is his greatest tone poem.

The Man Who Shot Liberty Valance is a political Western, a psychological murder mystery and John Ford's confrontation of the past – personal, professional and historical. The title itself suggests a multiplicity of functions. 'The man who' marks the traditional peroration of American nominating conventions, and has figured in the titles of more than fifty American films. In addition to evoking past time, 'shot' may imply a duel, a murder or an assassination. 'Liberty Valance' suggests an element of symbolic ambiguity. This is all *a priori*. After the film has unfolded, the title is reconstituted as bitter irony. The man who apparently shot *Liberty Valance* is not the man

175

The opening of *The Man Who Shot Liberty Valance* (James Stewart, Vera Miles, Andy Devine)

who really shot Liberty Valance. Appearance and reality? Legend and fact? There is that and more, although it takes at least two viewings of the film to confirm Ford's intentions and at least a minimal awareness of his career to detect the reverberations of his personality.

The opening sequences are edited with the familiar incisiveness of a director who cuts in the camera and hence in the mind. James Stewart and Vera Miles descend from a train which has barely puffed its way into the twentieth century. Their powdered make-up suggests that all the meaningful action of their lives is past. The town is too placid, the flow of movement too stately, and the sunlight bleaches the screen with an intimation of impending nostalgia. An incredibly aged Andy Devine is framed against a slightly tilted building which is too high and too fully constructed to accommodate the violent expectations of the genre. The remarkable austerity of the production is immediately evident. The absence of extras and the lack of a persuasive atmosphere forces the spectator to concentrate on the archetypes of the characters. Ford is well past the stage of the reconstructed documentaries (*My Darling Clementine*) and the visually expressive epics (*She Wore a Yellow Ribbon*). His poetry has been stripped of the poetic touches which once fluttered across the meanings and feelings of his art. Discarding all the surface artifices of realism, Ford runs the risk of seeming as lumberingly didactic as the late Renoir of *Le Déjeuner sur l'herbe* and the late

176

Dreyer of *Gertrud*. Ford's brush strokes of characterization seem broader than ever. Stewart's garrulous pomposity as the successful politician intensifies his wife's moody silence. She greets Andy Devine with a mournful intensity which introduces the psychological mystery of the film. Devine, Ford's broad-beamed Falstaff, must stand extra guard duty for the late Ward Bond and Victor McLaglen. Ford, the strategist of retreats and last stands, has outlived the regulars of his grand army.

Stewart seizes the opportunity to be interviewed by the local editor and staff, and entrusts his wife to Devine, who takes her in a buckboard to the ruins of a house in the desert. They sit in quiet, mysterious rapport until Devine descends to pick a wild cactus rose. Stewart is concluding his interview in the newspaper office when, through the window, the buckboard enters the frame of the film. We have returned to the compositional rigour of Stroheim's silent cinema in which the action invaded the rigid frame, and detail montage took it from there. But then Ford reverses the lateral direction of the film up to this point in order to lead his characters into an undertaker's shop, where they are reunited with Woody Strode, also artificially aged.

A man is lying in a coffin. We never see him, but we learn that his boots have been removed, that he is being buried without his gun belt and that, in fact, he has not worn his gun belt in years. Although we never see the corpse, we feel the presence of the man. The mood of irrevocable loss and stilled life becomes so oppressive that the editor (and the audience) demand an explanation. At a nod from his wife, Stewart walks into the next room away from the mourners, away from the present into the past. Just as Vera Miles begins to open her hat box, there is a cut to Stewart introducing the flashback by placing his hand on a historical prop, a dismantled, dust-ridden stagecoach. From the cut from the hat box to that climactic moment nearly two hours later when we see a cactus rose on the coffin, the cinema of John Ford intersects the cinema of Orson Welles. As Hitchcock and Hawks are directors of space, Ford and Welles are directors of time, the here and there, as it were, opposed to the then and now.

It is hardly surprising that the plot essence of the flashback is less important than the evocations of its characters. Whatever one thinks of *auteurism*, the individual films of John Ford are inextricably linked in an awesome network of meanings and associations. When we realize that the man in the coffin is John Wayne, the John Wayne of *Stagecoach, The Long Voyage Home, They Were Expendable, Fort Apache, She Wore a Yellow Ribbon, Rio Grande, Three Godfathers, The Quiet Man, The Searchers* and *Wings of Eagles*, the one-film-at-a-time reviewer's contention that Wayne is a bit old for an action plot becomes absurdly superficial. (Admittedly by 1975 Wayne's advanced age for action movies becomes a more valid issue.) *The Man Who Shot Liberty Valance* can never be fully appreciated except as a memory film, the last of its kind, perhaps, from one of the screen's old masters.

The first sequence of the flashback is photographed against a studio-enclosed skyscape far from the scenic temptations of the great outdoors. A stagecoach is held up almost entirely in close-up as if the action were being photographed inside a barn. Stewart, an idealistic dude lawyer from the East, gallantly defends Anna Lee, a Fordian lady since *How Green Was My Valley*, and is brutally flogged for his trouble by Liberty Valance, a hireling of the cattle interests. Indeed, Lee Marvin and his equally psychotic henchman (Strother Martin and Lee Van Cleef) convey an image of evil so intense that the film drifts into the Manichean conventions of horse opera. Curiously, Marvin, Martin and Van Cleef have grown in iconographical interest since 1962, Marvin as a fully fledged star in his own right, Martin as a Peckinpah standby and Van Cleef as Clint Eastwood's rival in the stirring spaghetti Westerns of Sergio Leone.

Ford, unlike Welles and Hitchcock, has never exploited Murnau's expressive camera movements which are capable of reversing moral relationships. Liberty Valance will be as much of a mad dog at the end as he is at the beginning. Every entrance he makes will be outrageous, but whip, gun and all, he represents something more than the pure villainy of the whining killers in *Wagonmaster*. As a political instrument of reactionary interests, Liberty Valance represents the intransigent individualism which Stewart is dedicated to destroy. Marvin and Wayne, however, are opposite sides of the same coin, and when Wayne kills Marvin to save Stewart for Vera Miles, he destroys himself. Burning down the house in the desert he had built for his bride, he is washed away by the stream of history. Wayne is seen for the last time walking away from a tumultuous convention about to nominate Stewart as the man who shot Liberty Valance.

The Man Who Shot Liberty Valance: intransigent individualism (John Wayne)

Ford's geography is etched in as abstractly as his politics. We are told that the cattle interests operate north of the picket line, but we never see the picket line,* and we never have a clear concept of the points of the compass. We are treated to a territorial convention without any explicit designation of the territory which is seeking statehood. (One may deduce one of the territories in the Southwest – Arizona or New Mexico – from the sympathetic presence of a Spanish-American contingent.) The alignment of farmers, merchants and townspeople against the ranchers is represented by scattered Ford types – Edmond O'Brien with the drunken eloquence of a newspaper editor sent west by Horace Greeley, John Qualen with the

---

* I am indebted to James D. Vizzini for his clarification of the geographical obscurity in the passage above: 'I think I've found a bit of Western trivia that clears up the ambiguity of locale in *The Man Who Shot Liberty Valance*. It is not a "picket line" that divides ranch empire and town (as you have written), but a "picket wire". And "the Picketwire" turns out to have been the cowboy bastardization of one Purgatoire River, which flows to this day in southeast Colorado.'

dogged tenacity of a Swedish immigrant, Ken Murray with the harsh fatalism of a frontier sawbones. Even lower on the credit roster one sees the familiar Ford gallery of scrambling humanity. There is still the same proportion of low humour, still disconcerting to some, derived from gluttony, drunkenness, cowardice and vainglory. Through the entire flashback Andy Devine fulfils his duties as town marshal by cowering behind doorways to avoid Liberty Valance. Yet Devine's mere participation in the fierce nobility of the past magnifies his character in retrospect. For Ford, there is some glory in just growing old and remembering through the thick haze of illusion.

Godard's neo-classical political collage in *Le Petit Soldat* is matched by Ford in a schoolroom scene in which Stewart is posed against a picture of Washington, and Woody Strode against a picture of Lincoln. Ford's obviousness transcends the obvious in the context of his career. For a director who began his career the year after Arizona and New Mexico were admitted to the Union, the parallel ambiguities of personal and social history project meanings and feelings beyond the immediate association of images. No American director has ranged so far across the landscape of the American past, the worlds of Lincoln, Lee, Twain, O'Neill, the three great wars, the western and transatlantic migrations, the horseless Indians of the Mohawk Valley and the Sioux and Comanche cavalries of the West, the Irish and Spanish incursions, and the delicately balanced politics of polyglot cities and border towns. There is the pastness also of Ford's own old movies, a pastness reflected in Wayne's first entrance in the film, on horseback, and adorned with the very tall hat of the earliest cowboy heroes. For a film historian with any kind of visual memory, the effect of Wayne's headgear is electrifying.

In accepting the inevitability of the present while mourning the past, Ford is a conservative rather than a reactionary. What he wishes to conserve are the memories of old values even if they have to be magnified into legends. The legends with which Ford is most deeply involved, however, are the legends of honourable failure, of otherwise forgotten men and women who rode away from glory towards self-sacrifice. In what is the last political assemblage Ford was to record, John Carradine, the vintage ham of the Ford gallery, matches his elocutionary talents on behalf of the cattle interests against Edmond O'Brien's more perceptive expression of a new civilization. When Carradine has concluded, a cowboy rides up the aisle and

180

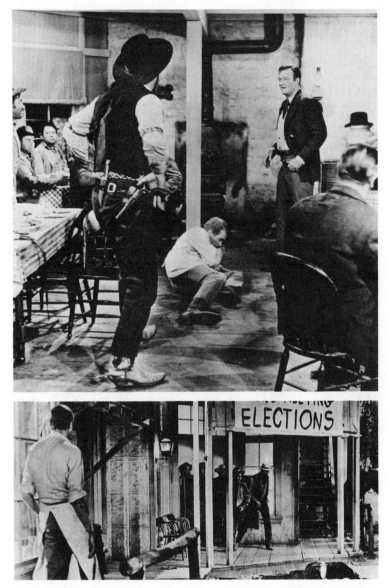

The Man Who Shot Liberty Valance: the making of a myth (Lee Marvin, James Stewart, John Wayne)

on to the speaker's rostrum to lasso the rancher's candidate with his good-natured complicity. This inspired bit of literal horseplay suggests a twinge of regret in the director's last hurrah for a lost cause. Shortly thereafter, Wayne strides out of the film past a forlorn campaign poster opposing statehood.

The shooting of Liberty Valance is shown twice from two different points of view. Kurosawa in *Rashomon* and Mankiewicz in *The Barefoot Contessa* have achieved an air of cynicism with this sort of subjective manoeuvre. Ford's juxtaposition of an action and its consequences from two different points of view is far more profound when the psychological chronology is properly assembled in the spectator's mind. The heroic postures of Wayne, Stewart and Marvin form a triangle in time. The conflicting angles, the contrasting plays of light and shadow, the unified rituals of gestures and movements and, above all, Ford's gift of sustained contemplation produce intellectual repercussions backwards and forwards in film time until, on a second viewing, the entire film, the entire world of John Ford, in fact, is concentrated into the first anguished expression of Vera Miles as she steps off the train at the beginning of the film, and everything that Ford has ever thought or felt is compressed into one shot of a cactus rose on a coffin photographed, needless to say, from the only possible angle.

Although *The Man Who Shot Liberty Valance* achieves greatness as a unified work of art with the emotional and intellectual resonance of a personal testament, there are enough shoulder-nudging 'beauties' in the direction to impress the most fastidious seekers of 'mere' technique. There is one sequence, for example, in which Edmond O'Brien addresses his own shadow as a forensic foreshadowing of a brutal beating he is about to receive, which might serve as a model of how the cinema can be imaginatively expressive without lapsing into impersonal expressionism. The vital thrust of Ford's actors within the bursting frames of his shot sequences demonstrates that life need not be devoid of form, and that form need not be gained at the expense of vitality. *The Man Who Shot Liberty Valance* must be ranked along with *Lola Montès* and *The Magnificent Ambersons* as one of the enduring masterpieces of that cinema which has chosen to focus on the mystical processes of time.

5: Epilogue

John Ford died on 31 August, 1973. Unlike D. W. Griffith and Buster Keaton, among many others, he did not die forgotten and unappreciated. Five months before his death he had been honoured by the American Film Institute with its first Life Achievement Award. In attendance had been the embattled President of the United States, and a thousand of Ford's friends and fellow professionals. My own modest contribution to that occasion was recorded in the AFI brochure for the ceremony:

John Ford might think it in bad taste even on this occasion for one of his admirers to note that so many of his films constitute a substantial body of sublime achievement in the cinema on this planet. Of course, Ford is especially sensitive to the great debt he owes all his friends and collaborators. If there is one idea above all others that has dominated what some call 'the world of his films' it is the idea of Community. It is an idea that glows through all his late films, and which, fittingly enough, glows also in the love and admiration tendered to him by all his friends and collaborators. He has never been afraid of the same old faces on the set and on the screen. He has always been too great and spiritual an artist to seek change through inconstancy. Hence, though all his films age, they never become dated. John Ford is not merely a man for all seasons, but an artist for all time.

Roger Greenspun wrote a thoughtful memorial tribute to Ford's total career in the *New York Times*. For his pains, Greenspun was attacked by several anti-Ford letter-writers in the weeks that followed. And so it has gone not only to the end, but even after the end.

Ford's career remains a controversial subject, despite the stirring tributes by Greenspun, Stuart Byron (*The Boston Real Paper*), Jon Landau (*Rolling Stone*), Joseph McBride and Peter Bogdanovich (*New York* magazine). This book was largely finished before Ford's death, and it was not originally conceived as a memorial. For my last words on John Ford, I turn to my 1966 *Village Voice* review of *Seven Women*, which turned out to be Ford's last film. I choose these last words precisely because they are not clouded over with grave-yard sentimentality. Indeed, they burn, perhaps excessively, with the white heat of polemical passion. More important, these words enable me to end this book at a transitional point in my quest for Ford's full meaning as a film-maker. Let it be said simply that the quest is just beginning, and that *Seven Women* marks as good a starting point as any.

John Ford's *Seven Women* has caused a slight stir in the trade by opening on the bottom half of a double bill with Burt Kennedy's *The Money Trap*, by all odds the daily double of the decade. My critical colleagues were more pitying than scornful as they confronted this latest opus of a director who has been in the business for more than fifty years. Some of them know how I loved and admired John Ford and tried to break the news to me gently. Ford, after all, was now past 70, and perhaps it was time to put the old war horse out to pasture. Ford's premature burial crew had the advantage of me because Metro had neglected to invite me to its screenings several months ago, and I had to wait for the not-so-grand opening on good old 42nd Street. Even so, I had braced myself for the worst. *Cheyenne Autumn* had been a failure, a noble failure, but a failure. Ford was never able to get inside his stone-faced Indians, and his best scene, the Wyatt Earp episode, had been truncated by the studio. Besides, what was one failure more or less in a career that has soared to so many new peaks? Ford has passed the point where he has to pay any instalments on his place in the Pantheon. His standing would not be jeopardized if he chose to direct the Three Stooges in a nudist movie, much less seven actresses in a Chinese adventure.

I could have saved my defensive rationalizations. *Seven Women* is a genuinely great film from the opening credit sequence of Mongolian cavalry massing and surging in slashing diagonals across the screen to Anne Bancroft's implacable farewell to Mike Mazurski's

Mongolian chieftain: 'So long, you bastard.' No lingeringly bitter tea of General Yen for Ford.

Not that I blame Metro for releasing *Seven Women* as unobtrusively as it did. The movie is at once too profound for the art-film circuit, and too personal for the big, brassy Broadway houses. Ford's films are passing into history and legend, and the veteran director may have heard his last hurrah. No matter. The beauties of *Seven Women* are for the ages, or at least for a later time when the personal poetry of film directors is better understood between the lines of genre conventions. Ford's gravest crime is taking his material seriously at a time when the seriousness of an entire medium is being threatened by the tyranny of trivia.

Seven Women is not being defended here because it is an old-fashioned kind of fun movie, outstanding solely for its outrageousness. Far from it. Ford represents pure classicism of expression in which an economy of means yields a profusion of effects. No one will ever catch John Ford at the Paris Cinémathèque studying *nouvelle vague* techniques. There is not a single jump cut or freeze frame in *Seven Women*. Nor are there any coy asides to the audience. Nor any concessions to 'modernity'. But then it would never occur to Ford, as it has to De Sica, to masquerade as a Great Director in search of the mass audience. Ford does not need to masquerade when any of his compositions selected at random will reveal an attention to nuanced detail and overall design such as to make a directorial monstrosity like *The Spy Who Came in from the Cold* look cinematically illiterate. Whereas Ritt ruins a trial scene with excessive cutting and unimaginative camera placement, Ford sustains psychological tensions with almost no interior literary support. Hence, Ford gets more drama out of a darkened hallway than Ritt can get out of a whole restaurant. There is one sequence in which Bancroft simultaneously surrenders her body and asserts her authority simply by striding towards the camera and forcing three people to react to her movement within the same frame. This movement triggers a series of abrupt actions with explosive force. When Ford finally does cut back and forth between Bancroft and Mazurski, the Eisensteinian collision is supplemented by a suppler sensibility capable of transmitting a touch of tenderness between two deadly antagonists.

Some critics have ridiculed the casting of Mazurski as a

Seven Women: (*above*) 'a configuration of Ford's vision of order'; (*opposite*) a sacrifice for survival (Anne Bancroft, Mike Mazurski)

Mongolian chieftain. Mazurski, like Ford's Negro giant regular Woody Strode, is cast less as a realistic Mongolian than as a fantasy male. Here we have seven women stranded in a Protestant mission in China in 1935. They have virtually excluded men from their sanctuary, and yet when the men swarm down on them, they are the worst kind of males the female psyche can envisage. These rampaging males wander around the countryside, raping, killing, plundering, and, worst of all, smashing all the windows, furniture and bric-à-brac. They affront every canon of order imposed upon the male by the female since the beginning of time, and yet the seven women must somehow come to terms with this monstrous maleness to survive, and a sacrifice must be made, a sordid sacrifice, it would seem, in the mere telling of the story, but a sublime sacrifice in Ford's filming.

The actresses – Anne Bancroft, Margaret Leighton, Betty Field, Sue Lyon, Flora Robson, Anna Lee and Mildred Dunnock – constitute a configuration of Ford's vision of order. It is interesting to speculate on what Patricia Neal would have been like in the part

Seven Women: the last farewell (Anne Bancroft, Mildred Dunnock)

Bancroft took over for the stricken Neal, but Bancroft is admirably forceful and direct, perhaps closer to the Manchus than to the Method, and perhaps all for the better. Ford's vision is open to criticism. He obviously finds women incomplete without men, but he nevertheless admires their gallantry and generosity and courage. In the end, women like men must submit to some order. The merits of the order are irrelevant, and here Ford leans more to the right in opposition to a Brecht who distinguishes between good and bad orders.

If Ford is not as fashionable as Brecht, however, it is simply because not as much has been written in the right places about distancing in cinema as there has been about distancing in theatre. The same fur-coated audiences sitting patiently at Lincoln Centre before the extravagant adventures of *The Caucasian Chalk Circle* would hoot at *Seven Women* with its infinitely subtler 'distancing'. The fake Metro set and sky, and the arbitrariness of the plot, are the materials of one of the cinema's greatest poets, though he would be the last to say so himself.

Filmography

The most comprehensive index of Ford's career published so far is the annotated filmography in Peter Bogdanovich's *John Ford*, an invaluable reference book for my own very speculative study. Considerations of space, common sense and borderline ethics make it more practical to provide a checklist of film titles here, and refer more detailed inquiries to Bogdanovich's book. I have italicized the titles of Ford films with more than esoteric interest for the general reader and moviegoer. I have not italicized any of Ford's silent films because the context of this part of his career is still unclear.

Films

1917 – The Tornado, The Scrapper, The Soul Herder, Cheyenne's Pal, Straight Shooting, The Secret Man, A Marked Man, Bucking Broadway. 1918 – The Phantom Riders, Wild Women, Thieves' Gold, The Scarlet Drop, Hell Bent, A Woman's Fool, Three Mounted Men. 1919 – Roped, The Fighting Brothers, A Fight for Love, By Indian Post, The Rustlers, Bare Fists, Gun Law, The Gun Packer, Riders of Vengeance, The Last Outlaw, The Outcasts of Poker Flat, The Ace of the Saddle, The Rider of the Law, A Gun Fightin' Gentleman, Marked Men. 1920 – The Prince of Avenue A, The Girl in Number 29, Hitchin' Posts, Just Pals. 1921 – The Big Punch, The Freeze Out, The Wallop, Desperate Trails, Action, Sure Fire, Jackie. 1922 – Little Miss Smiles, The Village Blacksmith. 1923 – The Face on the Barroom Floor, Three Jumps Ahead, Cameo Kirby, North of Hudson Bay, Hoodman Blind. 1924 – The Iron Horse, Hearts of Oak. 1925 – Lightnin', Kentucky Pride, The Fighting Heart, Thank You. 1926 – The Shamrock Handicap, The Blue Eagle, 3 Bad Men. 1927 – Upstream. 1928 – Mother Machree, Four Sons, Hangman's House, Napoleon's Barber, Riley the Cop. 1929 – Strong Boy, The Black Watch, Salute. 1930 – *Men Without Women*, Born Reckless, *Up the River*. 1931 – Seas Beneath, The Brat, *Arrowsmith*. 1932 – *Air Mail*, Flesh. 1933 – *Pilgrimage*, Dr Bull. 1934 – *The Lost Patrol*, The World Moves On, *Judge Priest*. 1935 – *The Whole Town's Talking, The Informer, Steamboat 'Round the Bend*. 1936 – *The Prisoner of Shark Island*, Mary of Scotland, The Plough and the Stars. 1937 – *Wee Willie Winkie, The Hurricane*. 1938 – Four Men and a Prayer, Submarine Patrol. 1939 – *Stagecoach, Young Mr Lincoln*, Drums Along the Mohawk. 1940 – *The Grapes of Wrath, The Long Voyage Home*. 1941 – Tobacco Road, Sex Hygiene (Army training film), *How Green Was My Valley*. 1942 – *The Battle of Midway* (war documentary). 1943 – December 7th, We Sail at Midnight (war documentaries). 1945 – *They Were Expendable*. 1946 – *My Darling Clementine*. 1947 – The Fugitive. 1948 – *Fort Apache*, Three Godfathers. 1949 – *She Wore a Yellow Ribbon*. 1950 – When Willie Comes Marching Home, *Wagonmaster, Rio Grande*. 1951 – This Is Korea! 1952 – What Price Glory?, *The Quiet Man*. 1953 – *The Sun Shines Bright, Mogambo*. 1955 – *The Long Gray Line*,

189

Mister Roberts (completed by Mervyn LeRoy), The Bamboo Cross (television film), Rookie of the Year (television film). 1956 – *The Searchers*. 1957 – *The Wings of Eagles, The Rising of the Moon*. 1958 – *The Last Hurrah*. 1959 – *Gideon of Scotland Yard* (G.B.: *Gideon's Day*), Korea (Defense Department documentary), *The Horse Soldiers*. 1960 – The Colter Craven Story (television film), *Sergeant Rutledge*. 1961 – *Two Rode Together*. 1962 – *The Man Who Shot Liberty Valance*, Flashing Spikes (television film), How the West Was Won (Multi-sequence film with other episodes directed by Henry Hathaway and George Marshall). 1963 – *Donovan's Reef*. 1964 – Cheyenne Autumn. 1965 –Young Cassidy (Jack Cardiff directed from Ford plan after Ford became ill). 1966 – *Seven Women*.

Select Bibliography

Books

Balshofer, Fred J., and Miller, Arthur C. *One Reel a Week*. Berkeley, University of California Press, 1967. pp. 183–88, 195–99.

Baxter, John. *The Cinema of John Ford*. New York, A. S. Barnes and Co. (The International Film Guide Series), 1971.

Bogdanovich, Peter. *John Ford*. Berkeley, University of California Press, 1968.

Fenin, George N., and Everson, William K. *The Western from Silents to Cinerama*. New York, Orion Press, 1962.

French, Warren. *Filmguide to* The Grapes of Wrath. Bloomington, Indiana University Press, 1973.

Haudiquet, Philippe. *John Ford*. Paris, Editions Seghers (Cinéma d'Aujourd'hui, no. 46), 1966.

McBride, Joseph, and Wilmington, Michael. *John Ford*. London, Secker and Warburg, 1975.

Mitry, Jean. *John Ford*. Paris, Editions Universitaires (Classiques du Cinéma, no. 1–2), 1954.

Pechter, William S. 'A Persistence of Vision', in *Twenty-four Times a Second: Films and Film-makers*. New York, Harper and Row, 1971. pp. 226–41.

Wollen, Peter. 'The Auteur Theory', in *Signs and Meaning in the Cinema*. London, Secker and Warburg (*Cinema One* series, no. 9), 1969. pp. 74–115.

Periodicals

Action (Directors Guild of America), vol. 6, no. 5 (Sept.–Oct., 1971). 'Special Issue devoted to John Ford and his towering achievement, *Stagecoach*.'

Cahiers du Cinéma, no. 45 (March, 1955), pp. 3–9. 'Rencontre avec John Ford' by Jean Mitry. (Reprinted in English in Andrew Sarris, ed., *Interviews with Film Directors*. New York, Bobbs–Merrill, 1967.)

Cahiers du Cinéma, no. 183 (October, 1966), pp. 38–70. 'Special John Ford' with filmography, interview, articles.

Cinema (Beverly Hills), vol. 6, no. 3 (Spring, 1971), pp. 21–36. 'John Ford' by Lindsay Anderson.

Film Comment, vol. 7, no. 3 (Autumn, 1971). pp. 8–23. Articles on Ford's late films.

Filmkritik, no. 181 (January, 1972). Entire issue devoted to 'John Ford's Stock Company'.

Films in Review, vol. 15, no. 6 (June–July, 1964), pp. 321–32. Report, with frequent quotes from Ford, on symposium held at UCLA as tribute to him.

Focus on Film, no. 6 (Spring, 1971). Issue devoted to Ford.

191

Présence du Cinéma, no. 21 (March, 1965), pp. 1–55. John Ford issue.
Sequence, no. 14 (New Year 1952), pp. 23–27. 'The Quiet Man', an interview with Lindsay Anderson.
Velvet Light Trap, no. 2 (August, 1971). John Ford issue.

Films

Directed by John Ford, by Peter Bogdanovich for the American Film Institute (1971).
The American West of John Ford, by Denis Sanders for CBS (1971).

Acknowledgments

I wish to thank William K. Everson, Eileen Bowser, Mark Segal, Peter Bogdanovich and Mel Asch for enabling me to see many of the Ford films first-hand. I am indebted to the insights into Ford's art revealed in the criticism, correspondence and conversation of Tom Allen, Stuart Byron, Richard Corliss, Stephen Gottlieb, Roger Greenspun, Stephen Harvey, Molly Haskell, Joseph McBride, Michael McKegney, William Paul, Robert Regan, Charles Silver, Peter Wollen, and the late Eugene Archer, who should have written this book a long time ago.

Stills by courtesy of Columbia, MGM, Paramount, RKO, 20th Century-Fox, United Artists, Universal, Warner Bros., and the Stills Library of the National Film Archive, London.